PROPOSALS FOR
A NEW SEXUAL ETHIC

JACK DOMINIAN

D0301245

Darton, Longman & Todd
London

First published in 1977 by
Darton, Longman & Todd Ltd
85 Gloucester Road, London SW7 4SU

© Dominian, 1977

ISBN 0 232 51379 1

Printed in Great Britain by the Anchor Press Ltd
and bound by Wm Brendon & Son Ltd,
both of Tiptree, Essex

CONTENTS

PREFACE

This book is made up of five articles which appeared in the Tablet, a Roman Catholic weekly, further expanded by four additional chapters. I remain, as always, grateful to the Editor of the Tablet, Mr T. Burns for publishing the articles and for allowing their reproduction in book form. The articles have been slightly modified by bringing together in the introduction, all references to the special position of the Roman Catholic Church.

My special thanks are also owed to my publisher and my wife for assisting me in the speedy preparation for publication.

Jack Dominian
Rickmansworth, Jan. 1977

INTRODUCTION

In a previous book *The Church and the Sexual Revolution*[1], a series of articles, which first appeared in the Tablet, introduced the challenge facing Christianity to consider afresh the theology of sexuality in terms of inter-personal relationships. Relationships which respond positively to God's precious gift of the attraction between the sexes lead to a union between a particular man and woman and form a community of love designated as marriage. The book aroused widespread interest and an increasing concern remains which is expressed in recurrent questions and enquiries in lectures, seminars and letters from this country and abroad. This interest has taken two forms, namely the desire to develop specific issues of the theology of sex, and secondly to consider such a development in the light of the official teaching of the Roman Catholic Church, in its encyclical Humanae Vitae and in the recent Declaration on Sexual Ethics.

Thus two issues are involved, first the evolution of sexual ethics as a concern of the *whole* Christian community and secondly, the special problems relating to the Roman Catholic Church. The controversies surrounding the specific teaching of the latter have at times tended to overshadow the much greater issues which involve all Christians and, in the further series of essays presented in this book, there is a deliberate policy to avoid controversy and instead to concentrate on developing and clarifying the previous work, presenting a new way of conceptualising sexual morality in its various stages of human development.

A sexual morality is outlined which has as its basis the concept of person, in terms of human wholeness, and love, conceived in terms of an ideal which seeks in sexual expression to involve as much of oneself and to interact with as much of the whole person of the other as is possible. The traditional concepts of permanency, faithfulness, creativity and life are expressed *anew* in psychological terms of interaction between persons expressing authentic love.

Seen in this new concept, many aspects of traditional sexual morality have to be examined afresh. At this point the severe critic will proclaim that no change is possible because Christian teaching is based on a combination of scriptural teaching and tradition which between them have already done full justice to human experience. Any 'development' is thus dismissed a priori as having only one possible source, the exaltation of the flesh and sexual pleasure as against self-discipline, control and asceticism. On this assumption any view which does not conform in the minutest detail to traditional teaching is seen as a deliberate deviation based on tempting the Christian community one step nearer the evils of the permissive society. The answer to this objection is a request to read carefully, without any previous assumptions, the text. Everything that is written in the following chapters eschews permissiveness with the same zeal as the most ardent critics. At the same time it is written with the conviction that Christian moral teaching is a constantly developing dialogue between an unfolding human experience and God's self-disclosure in the scriptures and tradition. Human experience is, of course, vital because social and psychological changes in society influence it profoundly and the unceasing seeking of human perfection which reflects the perfection in God ('You must therefore be perfect just as your heavenly Father is perfect'. Matt. 5,48) can only be achieved if humanity's deepening consciousness of itself, in terms of woman's emancipation, the man-woman relationship, the growing control over fertilisation, the reduction of the family size and the seeking of a deeper layer of personal fulfilment, is recognised, correctly appraised and expressed in a Christian morality that reflects and does justice to human integrity.

It is apt to quote here from one of the most important books on Marriage by Schillebeeckx [2] 'We should be wasting our time if we were to stand still, rapt in envious admiration of the past. We can feel nothing but respect and admiration when we look around and see how the modern family, despite the isolation and vulnerability to which it is subject, is able to achieve such depth in interpersonal relationships – practically the only buttress left to support the entire building. I do not believe those preachers who see nothing but materialism and egoism in the life of families today.'

Sharing the same optimistic attitude, it is my conviction that the social and psychological changes can, when considered in the light of Christian thought, deepen the image of God in man. 'God created man in the image of himself, in the image of God he created him, male and female he created them.' Gen. 1,27.

ROMAN CATHOLICISM

Authoritarianism

In this book specific views are expressed which run contrary to the current teaching of the Roman Catholic Church and it is important, in order to avoid misunderstandings, to state unequivocally my position in this matter. First of all the matter of authority has to be considered. A recurrent view expressed by a small minority within the Church is that whatever an author may say, if he or she is critical of any aspect of the Church's teaching, then by definition not only is he betraying the Church but he has no right to call himself a Roman Catholic. From time to time such views reach frenzied proportions and are expressed in similar exaggerated terms which respect neither logic nor the expressed intentions of the author. I have discussed the psychological inferences to be drawn from such attitudes in another book, *Authority*[3]. Often the very same people who are so critical betray their rigidity and disobedience in other matters. But in general these self-appointed critics are not concerned with the subject matter which they seem rarely to comprehend or to attend to objectively. Their only anxiety is that authority has been challenged. The good of Christianity and the Church is immaterial. All that matters is that the word of authority is blindly obeyed.

Such people have little understanding of genuine obedience or authority. They are authoritarian personalities whose bitter outbursts emanate from the depths of their personality out of fear. What they are concerned to preserve is a system of authoritarian order in which security is maintained by buttressing and idealising those in authority, through whom their own identity survives. What they are concerned with, and this is unconscious, is their own psychological and social survival, which is maintained by ensuring that authority preserves an order of clarity and safety in which they participate because they are unable to survive out of their own resources. Their emptiness is filled by blind obedience to authority and, if this or the institution from which it emanates is questioned, their source of strength and meaning is endangered and their emptiness threatens to overwhelm them.

The Catholic Church, like any other institution, has its share of such people, both lay and religious, and they retain an unceasing vigilance as they believe for the good of the Church, but in reality for their own badly needed security which is threatened by any change and doubly threatened when the supreme authority of the Church is subjected to any questioning. They often accuse their 'victim' of attacking the Holy Father, damaging the Church, being no longer worthy of the name of Roman Catholic and in the process they act with no respect for truth, justice or fidelity to the ideas of those they attack. But then these people have no time for ideas. Their motivation is entirely psychological and unconscious and springs from fear. Other people's ideas are for them intolerable threats and all they want to achieve is to eliminate these threats by *any* means.

But even those who neither *feel* nor react like this *feel* uncomfortable when the Church's teaching is questioned in major issues. It is therefore important to spell out what I understand by authority and obedience. The Roman Catholic Church is so structured that in matters of faith and morals 'Bishops, teaching in communion with the Roman Pontiff, are to be respected by all as witnesses to divine and Catholic truth. In matters of faith and morals, the bishops speak in the name of Christ and the faithful are to accept their teaching and adhere to it with a religious assent of soul. This religious submission of will and mind must be shown in a special way to the authentic teaching authority of the Roman Pontiff, even when he is not speaking ex cathedra. That is it must be shown in such a way that his supreme magisterium is acknowledged with reverence, the judgements made by him are sincerely adhered to, according to his manifest mind and will.' [4]

If we examine this text of Vatican II carefully, and it is a favourite of those who wish to use it as a stick to beat any deviance as they see it, what are its critical constituents? First of all it is clear that no one can proclaim obedience and adherence to the Church if he or she were to deny the basic structure and claims of the bishops and the pope. If their authority to teach is denied, then there is no point in pretending to be a Roman Catholic. There is, of course, much interest in how the subject matter which is taught is actually formulated. Further we must distinguish between the authority to teach and how the conclusions of what is taught are reached. These are issues which concern the whole Church and theologians in particular examine them carefully. Nevertheless when a declaration has been made, even if it is not ex cathedra, i.e. is not infallible[5], it is required that the teaching is treated with reverence and adhered to as the authentic teaching of the Church, which in turn, of course, reflects the acknowledgement of the supreme position of the Pope and the bishops as teachers.

In all my writings I have adhered to all these criteria and I challenge anyone to show that I have not maintained strictly that until the present teaching is altered, it remains the basis from which any moral decision must be taken by a Roman Catholic. This teaching cannot be abrogated by me or anyone else because no individual has such authority in the Roman Catholic Church. Nor is there any doubt in my mind that the teaching of Humanae Vitae and the Declaration on Sexual Ethics springs from the deepest concern of the Holy Father and his advisors to guide the faithful on this topic in these difficult days. His motives deserve and require absolute respect and this has never been denied by me. What happens, however, when there is profound disagreement about the best means of preserving Christian love within sexuality?

This is an issue which has faced the Church since its inception, namely the presence of genuine disagreement about the truth and its interpretation. First of all a genuine disagreement does not necessarily imply an attack on the teaching authority of the Church. If it did, there would never be any means of developing moral thought and clearly such development has occurred. It is particularly important to mention this because so much of the opposition to Humanae Vitae was not really concerned directly with the evolution of sexual ethics; rather the encyclical provided a focal point to express all kinds of rebellious feelings at a time when the Church was experiencing its first stage of absorbing the changes introduced by Vatican II. To equate disagreement with rebellion or the desire to destroy the Church is an incredibly naive interpretation of reality and the history of the Church. It is true that, amongst those who have disagreed and are likely to disagree in the future with the teaching authority of the Church, there will be a number who will ultimately break away in a fundamental manner. Equally many more have remained loyal and have influenced profound changes. What really matters is the motivation of the people concerned and the motivation of this author is the good of the Church and the pursuit of truth.

The Laity

The Council not only reaffirms the authority of the Pope and the bishops but has emphasised in a new and vital way the role of the laity. 'Every layman should openly reveal to them (sacred pastors) his needs and desires with that freedom and confidence which befits a son of God and a brother of Christ.' [6] These words have a particular significance for me. Ultimately, if we are to take the Church seriously as mature adults and not as frightened children clothed in adult uniforms, then we must see it as a Christian community where trust, love and sincere intentions are clearly discerned and fostered both when they express agreement or disagreement with authority. Public compliance coupled with private indifference or neglect destroy the credibility of the Christian community and the Roman Catholic Church has suffered too much from such incompatibility. 'An individual layman, by reason of the knowledge, competence or outstanding ability which he may enjoy, is permitted and sometimes even obliged to express his opinion on things which concern the good of the whole Church. When occasions arise, let this be done through the agencies set up by the Church for this purpose. Let it always be done in truth, in courage and in prudence, with reverence and charity towards those who by reason of their sacred office represent the person of Christ.' [7] It is my sincere belief expressed over a number of years in several publications[8] that the present teaching on sexual ethics needs a profound Christian revaluation and that some features of specific Roman Catholic teaching need alteration. If specific authority to express this view is required, it is to be found in the text just quoted.

It is up to readers to judge whether I possess the necessary credentials and whether the presentation has been made with prudence, reverence and charity towards authority but that has always been my intention not because I fear to offend or intend subtly to destroy but because of the way I understand and have experienced the Church. I have found that its priests and bishops whom I know personally are my neighbours in Christ who I both respect because of their office but even more with whom I agonise because I know that they care about the truth and the well-being of their flock. I have no personal knowledge of the Holy Father but I am sure he cares and agonises as well. Thus it is love and not fear that prompts all I have to say and the way that I say it, and in love mistakes are made but can be absorbed by it.

Nevertheless ultimately it is the truth that matters and all that is written here is offered for serious discussion and commentary[9, 10]. If space has been taken to clarify the Roman Catholic position, this has been done to eliminate unnecessary misunderstandings and so concentrate on the ideas offered. In the end the whole Christian community has to evaluate the views presented and it will be up to the teaching authority of the Church to consider them. This will take time. Ideas about such basic issues do not alter quickly and much patience is required for several provisional conclusions. In the history of the Church ideas were sometimes discussed for centuries before the Church pronounced officially on a conclusion. Nowadays we need faster decisions but even so, when we are in the midst of such profound changes, care and prudence are essential.

The sexual life of the single person

At regular intervals I receive severe remonstrations for concentrating so much on the sexual ethics and love of the married and neglecting the sexual life of the single person. I recognise that this is the case and remains so in this book. The fact is that the single person can mean those in their adolescence, those who remain single in their twenties, thirties, forties and later on, the separated and divorced, the widows and widowers, those who chose the single state dedicated to God and a number of men and women with a mixture of some of these states. To do justice to the sexual ethics of the single person requires more than a superficial and generalised recognition of these states. Each of them has its own special characteristics which I hope to treat at length in another work.

Aim of the book

In conclusion, the aim of this book is to expand on the ideas first offered in *The Church and the Sexual Revolution* and to

16

develop a new and systematic approach to sexual ethics which concern the whole Christian community and in particular certain aspects of the teaching of the Roman Catholic Church.

The views expressed here are but one way of conceptualising the topic. There are others which will have to be considered before a new synthesis emerges. What is inescapable is that such a new revaluation is urgently needed, not as an expression of permissiveness but as a means of directing effectively the eternal vigilance and discipline required to sustain love. The world is as deeply hungry for genuine love as it is for a new understanding of God and as St John tells us the two equate 'because God is love' (John I 4,8.) Any genuine advance in our understanding of love can only further the illumination of the meaning of God at a time of unprecedented confusion about both.

This book is offered in the sincere hope that it will, however minutely, advance the cause of the two most precious realities that man experiences and to which he responds, namely God and love.

NOTES

1. Dominian J. 1971 *The Church and the Sexual Revolution*. Darton, Longman and Todd, London.
2. Schillebeeckx E. 1976 *Marriage*. Sheed and Ward, Stagbooks.
3. Dominian J. 1976 *Authority*. Burns and Oates, London.
4. *The Documents of Vatican II* 1967, Dogmatic Constitution on the Church Chap III Section 25.
5. Rahner K. and Vorgrimler H. *Concise Theological Dictionary*. Burns and Oates p. 228.
6. See 4 Chap 14 Section 37.
7. As above.
8. a) See 1.
   b) Dominian J. 'Birth Control and Married Love.' The Month March 1973.
9. Those who find it very difficult to conceive of change in dogmatic pronouncements should refer to the statement by the Sacred Congrega-

tion for the Doctrine of Faith in 1973 which states clearly the strength and weakness of dogmatic infallible assertions, summarised by R. E. Brown in the Tablet (15.1.1977) when he states 'doctrinal affirmations are frequently incomplete, limited by the outlook of the human beings who shaped them and by the questions they meant to answer and, above all, enunciated in terms that bear traces of "the changeable conceptions of a given epoch".' That means that any new formulation of truth can never be completely dismissed ab initio simply by repetition of past church statements. (Neither Humanae Vitae nor the Declaration on Sexual Ethics are of course definite infallible declarations.)

10. For further extensive treatment of the same issue by a leading theologian see the article by J. Fuchs, The absoluteness of Moral Terms, a German text published simultaneously in the volume Testimonium Veritate (J. Knecht, Frankfurt–Main) and in English in Gregorianum Vol 52 Fasc3.

I

CHRISTIANS AND SEX

Twelve years ago the Vatican II council ended. The manifold issues facing the Roman Catholic Church since then have been described with rare excellence in Hebblethwaite's book, *The Runaway Church*.[1] Much of the discussion regarding the post-conciliar church is of particular concern for those Catholics and Christians of other denominations who are constantly comparing the Church as they knew it before the Council and the Church of today. However, there is emerging with increasing force a Church, mostly of young people, who know very little about the pre-conciliar Church, who are in many ways different types of Christians and Roman Catholics. For them, many of the familiar arguments are boring, obsolete and irrelevant. They are conscious of totally new priorities which can be summed up first of all in their genuine difficulty in experiencing God, and secondly, when they do find this God, in identifying His presence in the love of personal relationships and in social justice in the community, the local one at home and the deprived abroad. Love in personal relationships and social justice dominate the minds of the emerging church as apologetics, obeying rules and regulations, authoritarian principles and the salvation of one's soul dominated the minds of a previous generation. For this emerging generation of believers, God's presence is to be acknowledged not only directly through prayer, liturgy and the sacraments, but even more emphatically through the

19

righteousness of living in the community of personal relationships and the wider community of peoples where the priority above all others is social justice between those who have and those who have not in terms of power, resources, equality, significance and opportunity in the realisation of human potential. It is not surprising that the previous criteria of the 'good practising' Catholic are diminishing by whatever objective measurement is made. A new Christian community is emerging but careful discernment is needed to identify it in the prevailing confusion, although islands of new meaning can be found just under the surface of this confusion. Perhaps the uncertainty is at its most marked in the field of sexuality which is such a vital component of personal relationships.

A decade of openness has made the subject of human sexuality much less of a taboo even within the Church, but the Roman Catholic Church, like the rest of the Churches and the secular community, goes on expressing the most profoundly contradictory positions in its attitude towards the subject. On the one hand, there exists the most revolutionary and promising statement on marriage and the family in the documents of Vatican II, on the other there have been two most traditional pronouncements regarding human sexuality, namely Humanae Vitae and the Declaration on Sexual Ethics, which have left most Roman Catholics, particularly the young, puzzled and frustrated. A great number of them are firmly convinced that in many specific areas the Church has simply lost control over this topic and that the principles guiding its two post-conciliar pronouncements are not only basically unsound but irrelevant. This chapter could be filled with detailed references to world wide disenchantment and concern regarding the Church's attitude to sexuality. No one would disagree that there is a real crisis. The ensuing debate would be about the nature of the crisis.

Some would see this as a straightforward crisis of authority. Their attitude would be that the Church has spoken in Humanae Vitae and in the Declaration and those who cannot accept this teaching cannot consider themselves to be 'good' Catholics, obedient to the voice of the Church. Those who hold this opinion would undoubtedly have predominantly

20

pre-conciliar habits of thought and for them there would be no other issue than that of obedience. Still remaining within the large majority of Catholics whose training and formation has been largely pre-conciliar, we would find those who, despite their conditioned training to accept the official teaching of the Church, would disagree to a variable degree with the contents of the pronouncements in this specific area of human sexuality.

New Insights

Finally, the new Church which is emerging, made up largely of young people but having a number of adherents from predominantly pre-conciliar trained Catholics, believes that the whole basis of Christian thinking on sexual morality needs fundamental reconstruction. Without any hesitation, I place myself in this category and will attempt in this and the following chapters to *outline* the basis of such a reconstruction. Some readers who have followed my writings for over a decade will feel and share with me the frustration that so little progress has been made in this fundamental area. The resistance to change has been immense, and this is not surprising when we consider that we are dealing with one of the most fundamental aspects of human behaviour. But delay and procrastination cannot go on for ever because the undeniable vacuum in Christian thought is being filled by alternative ideologies which have little respect for either Christian or human values. Furthermore, even within Catholic circles, it is fashionable to proclaim the autonomy of personal decisions based on conscience. Such personal decisions are, however, the subject of bitter controversy. Since the formulations of the council are such in certain topics that there is ample room to ally oneself with either pre-conciliar or post-conciliar theological positions, those who object to the greater freedom given to personal decisions based on conscience insist that conscience must still be informed by the teaching of the Church and that this means, in sexual ethics, carrying out the letter of the law of Humanae Vitae and the Declaration. Those who rely on the

21

greater freedom of personal decision based on conscience find themselves with precious little moral consensus on such matters as the significance of sexual pleasure, masturbation, pre-marital sexual intercourse, contraception, divorce and the crisis of love.

Thus, the crisis is not one primarily of obedience but of the breakdown of a consensus of appropriate moral value systems. In the absence of such a consensus, situational ethics flourish. But the target for criticism should be neither situational ethics, nor the flexibility of moral decisions. Rather it should be the absence of an appropriate revaluation of sexual morality and if blame has to be apportioned, it is the Church which is responsible. Since the Church still very often means those in authority, it is only too easy to blame the Pope, the bishops, the priests and for good measure the teachers who perpetuate obsolete sexual value systems. Many will know by now that I, for one, do not find it easy to add my own to such accusing fingers. As a psychiatrist, I know only too well the incessant need we all have to find scapegoats, to project our own failures and limitations on others, and the Catholic Church with its powerful authoritarian structure lends itself to such self-justifying processes better than most. But when the dust of the mutual accusations has settled down, there still remains a crisis which has to be resolved by the *whole Christian community* and that means that lay men and women have to play an infinitely greater role in formulating new sexual principles. First, however we must point to some incontrovertible human changes which are fundamental and revolutionary and which make the alterations in sexual morality essential.

Life and Sexual Pleasure

Perhaps no idea is more deeply embedded in popular thought and moral theology than that sexual intercourse is legitimate within marriage only and that the pleasure of the act is intimately related to what used to be described until Vatican II as the primary end of marriage, namely procreation. Sex is pleasurable and that this pleasure is primarily linked with

22

children is a notion firmly established in both popular and traditional moral thinking. This is not the place to consider this notion in detail, but no-one will argue against it in its broadest sense. The opposite proposition is that sex is pleasurable in its own right, has little to do with marriage or procreation and should be pursued as an end in itself. This fundamental dichotomy with all its emotive overtones still governs much of the discussion on this topic. Thousands of polemic articles formulate this polarity which sees Christianity as an opponent of sexual pleasure, only concerned with procreation, and the rest as seeking an unfettered hedonism. There are so many reasons for discussing the matter in this way that few bother to see that such an argument presented in this way is largely irrelevant both for Christianity and everyone else.

The crucial fact remains that, with or without contraception, men and women have acquired so much control over the moment of fertilisation that virtually 99 per cent of sexual activity even within marriage will be knowingly non-procreative in the future. It is ironic that the Roman Catholic Church with its insistence on the infertile period has provided perhaps the single most important scientific contribution to the exact details of the life span of the ovum and the sperm, the time of ovulation and the possibilities of fertilisation. Much of the discussion on world population has focused on what the world can sustain in numbers as far as food is concerned. But at the personal level, we are moving into a completely new historic era, when fertilisation will come almost completely under man's control and therefore we are witnessing the end of the era which has linked sexual pleasure predominantly with procreation. No-one can evade this fundamental issue. We must seek an alternative meaning which will link life and sexual pleasure.

The Changing Status of Woman

Little needs to be said about the truth revealed in Genesis, namely that men and women were both created in the image

23

of God and that they are both one in Christ, confirming their equality of worth in the presence of complementary characteristics. 'There are no more distinctions between Jew and Greek, slave and free, male and female, but all of you are one in Christ Jesus' (Gal. 3,28). This is being both proclaimed and realised in different degrees in various parts of the world. The implications for the man-woman relationship in its physical, emotional and social dimensions are enormous. Christianity, with its marked androcentricity and a theology almost totally formulated by men, cannot claim to be ready to face the implications of such a transformation. It is symptomatic of the size of the issue that within the Catholic Church we are merely grasping at such issues as the celibacy of the priesthood and that other denominations are concerned with the ordination of women. The truth is that the whole world is facing a revolution in human relationships of unprecedented measure and Christianity must recognise that it is totally unprepared for these implications which will affect the whole order of social and psychological structures in society. In the sexual sphere, women in Western societies have already ceased to spend large parts of their lives in reproduction. They are rebelling against being mere objects of male sexual attraction and are seeking an equivalent degree of personal sexual fulfilment. Instead of facing the challenge of these changes, Catholics have been waging campaigns against them for decades, on the grounds that they are anti-life and a threat to family life. Until the inevitable and justifiable claims of women are recognised, no-one will pay the slightest attention to the genuine anti-life and anti-love elements in certain ideologies. Christianity will only be heard if it is seen to speak from a position of genuine equality of worth between the sexes. There is a most urgent need to formulate its theological basis.

Rising Expectations

A theology of sex which concentrated on procreation and the family can no longer do justice to the one or the other in a

24

world in which one third are seeking values which emphasise a much deeper layer of personal psychological and social fulfilment and two thirds are threatened by poverty and exploitation and are desperately seeking social justice. In both the developed and under-developed parts of the world for very different reasons, sex is no longer seen primarily as an agent of life in terms of the number of children but as a contributor to the quality of life in terms of personal relationships and social justice. In both these worlds contraception, sterilisation and other hitherto totally unacceptable practices are becoming common every-day events. In the past they could all be collectively condemned because of a very simple principle. All involved attendant sexual pleasure with the frustration of the end result of a possible fertilisation of ovum and sperm. The morality of condemnation has had an utter simplicity. Sexual pleasure was only legitimate within marriage and when the act remained open on every occasion to the possibility of new life. By making sexual pleasure and biological openness to life the key to all morality, the theologian had a simple task but as a result the Church has a theology of sexuality whose simplicity also tends towards naivety. Contraception, sterilisation, artificial insemination, masturbation and so on do in fact have in common the consequence of sexual pleasure, but the issues and personal implications involved are so totally different that a morality which has as its common and main denominator sexual pleasure or openness to biological life is totally unsatisfactory. This is part of the enormous challenge facing us in our re-formulation of sexual ethics; each topic will have to be treated in a separate fashion; but if one common factor is needed to influence moral principles, since when has love been a stranger in the Christian tradition for the basis of the formulation of moral laws? The shift from biology and physiology to person and love is a good beginning for the mammoth task ahead and one which is in keeping with the theology of Vatican II.

NOTE

1. Hebblethwaite P. 1975 *The Runaway Church*. Collins, London.

II

SEXUAL PLEASURE

Perhaps no greater need exists in the field of sexual morality than the restoration of significant value to sensual gratification and in particular sexual pleasure. Given the extensive and profound opposition from certain Christian writers,[1] this fundamental alteration in attitude will not be accomplished without great effort and care, but there can be little doubt that the Christian community as a whole is looking for a positive lead in this matter.

Historical Background

In a brief account of this type there is little space to review the complex and diverse attitudes to be found in the Old and the New Testament and the increasingly hostile elements which crept into the Christian tradition from the second century onwards culminating in the negative formulations of St Augustine. The basic positive tenets nevertheless remain and are to be found in Genesis in which God found all that He had created not only good but very good, and that must certainly include the experience of pleasure; in the Song of Songs which is a lyrical and exuberant exaltation of physical love; in the positive attitude to the permanent relationship betwen a man and a woman in marriage; in the innumerable references throughout the Scriptures to the dangers of physical beauty

27

which suggests that here exists a characteristic that has powerful positive and negative features for there would be no danger unless human beings are deeply involved in the experience. In other words physical pleasure and sexuality are intrinsic to the very essence of being human and such a characteristic deserves to be taken with the utmost seriousness in its positive personal significance and not to be permanently surrounded with fear, negativity, hostility and suspicion. This is not to say that a slow process of modification has not been taking place for a long time. But all the time the primary influence has been from outside the Christian community, reacting to the pressures of a pluralistic society, rebelling and questioning the values of Western society which have been predominantly Christian in nature. The recent post-war rebellion has been against the so called Victorian puritanism but this is only a transient historical phenomenon and the roots of the Christian enmity towards sexual gratification originate from virtually the very beginning of its historic establishment. Thus the process of rehabilitation needs to be far more fundamental than a mere reaction to an age. Christianity has to evolve its own value systems by examining the extensive information that has been acquired about the psychological development of the personality and the relationship of sensual gratification to love which is the basic guiding principle for a faith which claims that God is love.

Infantile Sexuality

Whilst not being the first, Freud was definitely the most prominent worker of the last hundred years who drew our attention to a dimension of childhood sensual gratification which has enduring effect during the rest of our lives. His initial theoretical model has been modified by successive workers but there remains a basic infrastructure that is clear and of vital significance in human relationships.

As is well known, Freud conceptualized a theory for the emergence of the adult personality which was based on the presence, development and ultimate control of two instincts, sexuality and aggression. His theories shocked his contemporaries not only by placing prominence on such taboo subjects as sex and aggression but also by focusing on the earliest years of our lives which had been considered sacrosanct and free from such 'impure' components. His essays on sexuality[2] which he wrote in 1905 opened a new era of originality and drew strong reaction. Three quarters of a century later they still cause much controversy but have undoubtedly revolutionised our thinking about the nature of man. This is not to say that his theories have gone unchallenged or that there have not been significant alterations and alternative views. Nevertheless there is a nucleus of his theory which remains invaluable in understanding the origin of instinctual gratification.

Freud postulated a sexual energy which he labelled the libido. Those who wish to have concrete, measurable, objective criteria find the idea of libido difficult to identify and indeed query the concept and its existence. Nevertheless its presence or absence does not nullify the theoretical framework which Freud described for the growth of the personality. He postulated that the young baby is a mass of instinctual needs which impinge on the personality in an ordered sequence of phases which he called the oral, the anal and the phallic. The theory goes well beyond this, suggesting that each stage of development is associated with specific characteristics of the personality but this is even more difficult to establish.

What is not difficult to perceive is that the child derives a great deal of satisfaction at the beginning of its life which is sensual in character and is located initially in the mouth. The satisfaction goes well beyond the satiation of hunger. The lips with their smooth lining and the mouth as a whole provide a specific sensuous feel which not only serves tasting and later on mastication (the original expression of oral aggression) but remain an important source of expressing and receiving physical pleasure through kissing and contact in various forms. Furthermore, although Christian writing usually recoils even from admitting this reality except occasionally in the past in the footnotes of Latin textbooks of moral theology, . the mouth is used not infrequently as an orifice for sexual intercourse or as an instrument of pleasure. Now this topic can and has been dismissed as pornographic and filthy and in this way persistently rendered unsuitable as a subject fit for legitimate discussion within the Christian framework of reference. On the other hand, if we start with the actual experience of a couple who find oral intercourse satisfying, then we may encounter not pornography, filth or degradation but a joy mutually shared. The reality cannot be denied. The value may be questioned, but it can only be dismissed by insisting that sexual intercourse can only take place in a specified manner. The answer as already indicated is validated because of the obvious biological penis-vagina connotation, but as will be repeatedly asserted, a morality of whole persons involves more than biology, it involves values of mutual joy, life and satisfaction. In this case there is ample evidence that some couples do find oral intercourse a satisfactory variant and certainly the Freudian model offers a satisfactory explanation for this existential reality.

The oral phase is followed by the anal. Freud postulated that the centre of sensation and pleasure which succeeds the mouth is the anus, a site lined with similar smooth membrane and capable like the mouth of providing physical pleasure during elimination. The sexual significance of the buttocks and the associated site of elimination, makes the whole area one of intense curiosity, disgust, sexual arousal and pleasure. Ordinary language has produced a rich terminology of sexual and excretory expressions, which once again have not been acknowledged or taken seriously in Christian thought. Since this is the every-day language and experience of the whole of mankind, Christian morality remains significantly at odds with the world and faces the same problem when the anal orifice is used as a site of sexual intercourse, heterosexually or homosexually. Once again the refusal to recognise the reality of the situation does not stop millions of men and women actually experiencing such sexual variants and finding pleasure, joy, satisfaction and fulfilment. They may equally find pain, disgust and repulsion in which case they do not repeat the experience. But, for those who find pleasure, the act is repeated even though it may be forbidden by law and certainly by the hitherto accepted morality. But in the privacy of their homes men and women express their love in the way they know is authentic and here as elsewhere Christianity can only become increasingly a centre of a conspiracy of silence if it does not consider openly the values inherent in such activity. Anal intercourse may be the predeliction of the few, the significance of the buttocks as an erotogenic area is, however, a universal experience which can be neither ignored nor dismissed and, even within the present moral categories, remains a legitimate source of excitation and pleasure. If Christianity is not to be seen as a religion inimical to human integrity, it has to recognise and face openly the ingredients of sexual pleasure placed by the Creator within the body and to leave behind for ever an attitude of trivialising those gifts of God to man which can become the springs of joy, pleasure and loving communion.

The oral and anal is followed in the Freudian framework by the phallic. Here the young child focuses on its genitals, the boy recognising the presence and significance of the penis and the girl its absence. Freud, despite his genius, expressed the same andro-centric bias as the rest of his age, made this phase which occurs about the fifth year an event of absence for the girl. The girl is supposed to notice an absence, a loss. We need not detain ourselves with this peculiar Freudian emphasis on the male supremacy but it is worth repeating here a point made elsewhere that in a strange way Freud and Christianity both collude in their respective emphasis on sex, the former by stressing its importance and making it a foundation pillar of the human personality, the latter by ignoring and under-valuing its significance for nearly two thousand years. Both collude by isolating its significance in personal relationship at the expense of love which is served by sexuality but which, undoubtedly, has the ultimate supreme value. Love has the capacity of involving the whole person, body, mind and feelings in personal affirmation and mutual love, whereas sex, either its exaltation or dismissal, has the capacity of reducing a person to a part, a danger of diminution and fragmentation of a whole.

Be that as it may, the phallic phase became for Freud the

pinnacle of the development of the human personality in the acting out of the Oedipus complex. By this complex Freud meant that the little boy is naturally attracted to his mother sexually but has to deny this infantile sexual demand and give way to father and the reverse for the little girl. In doing so, the boy begins to ally himself with father and assume the male identification (failure of which is considered to be one of the reasons for male homosexuality when the boy continues to identify with the mother) and the girl identifies with her mother and assumes the feminine makeup. Other more detailed and recent work places sexual identification in terms of gender and identity at a much earlier period.[2a] But Freud was the first worker to provide a comprehensive theory of sexual identity. After the Oedipal phase, there is a latent period which is brought to an end by puberty when sexual relationships have a specific genital dimension as well.

The Pleasure of Attachment

The Freudian model, with its overt sexual references to oral and anal erotogenic zones, provides a powerful barrier to acceptance because it involves some of our most powerful taboo conditioning. Christianity is a faith, however, which aims at the truth, the sort of truth that facilitates relationships of love between human beings and between men and women and God. It cannot afford the luxury of deliberately ignoring such a basic aspect of human encounter.

This chapter has so far described the pleasure of attachment in instinctual sexual terms, but such a description has not been left at the level of the original Freudian model. Analysts like K. Horney,[3] Erikson[4] and Bowlby,[5] have taken Freud's original thought and developed it further. Erikson, Bowlby, Winnicott[6] and others have all shown that the strictly Freudian model has to be expanded further.

The young baby arrives in this world as a helpless dependent being who needs to master incorporation, retention and elimination but also needs equally trust, security, approval, affection, in brief the ingredients of feeling recognised, wanted, appreciated and cherished. All this it experiences in its first two years of life through the body before language adds its specific contribution.

Security and trust are experienced through the body. The mother, or reliable mother substitute, conveys to the baby sensations of proximity, safety, warmth, acknowledgement, the soothing of anxiety, the removal of pain, the joy of laughter and play. All this is primarily conveyed through touch, aided and abetted by vision and sound. The child's eyes are constantly searching for the presence of the loving object, mother, and the meeting of their mutual gaze fortifies presence, safety, acknowledgement, acceptance. If mother cannot be seen, her presence can be verified through the sound of her voice and her movements. Her voice is a major contributor of joy and reassurance.

In brief touch, vision, sound and smell between them become a powerful signalling system for attachment and bonding; they become the infrastructure of personal recognition, friendship and loving relationships throughout life. Here we reach a vital point which needs detailed attention and clarification. The experiences of touching, watching, talking and listening are the foundations of physical intimacy, the infrastructure of human attachment and therefore of affection. Later on after puberty the very same experiences will be capable of arousing not only affection but also sexual desire. Furthermore sexual arousal can now occur in the absence of any personal attachment, friendship or love. It can be simply a sexual drive or in other terms a lustful longing without any bonds of affection towards the person with whom the sexual arousal is experienced.

There is little doubt in my mind that here is the key to the fear attached to human sexuality, namely the severance at puberty between genital sex and any necessary personal attachment to the object of the sexual arousal, the essence of prostitution and one of the symbols in the Old Testament of Israel's unfaithfulness to Yahweh. No-one denies this crucial human predicament but because it exists there is no reason to devalue either human affection or sexuality in the presence of a loving relationship. In particular human affection as expressed through looks, touch and language becomes the most powerful means of initiating and sustaining bonds of friendship and affection. Indeed they play a vital role in all human relationships where bonds are not primarily sexual in character. It is part of the mature development of every man and woman to be able to separate an intimacy of friendship from sexual arousal; in all their human relationships, the celibates, the single and the married, must be able to distinguish and express to each other these various forms of affection, the foundations of which were laid in the first few years of our life.

One cannot over-emphasise that neither the frightened obsessional preoccupation which has made Christian circles treat bodily encounter with utter apprehension nor the opposite of utter abandonment to bodily experience do justice to human integrity which must always use the body as an instrument of love but discriminate the expression that is appropriate for the specific relationship of the individual couple or group of persons.

NOTES

1. Bailey D. S. 1959 *The Man-Woman Relation in Christian Thought*. Longmans
2. Freud S. 1905 *Three Essays on the Theory of Sexuality*, Vol III
2a. R. J. Stoller 1968 *Sex and Gender*. Hogarth Press, London
3. Horney K. 1937 *The Neurotic Personality of our times*. W. W. Norton and Co. Inc. New York
4. Erikson E. H. 1968 *Identity*. Faber, London
5. Bowlby J. 1969 *Attachment and Loss*. Hogarth Press, London
6. Winnicott D. W. 1965 *The Maturational Processes and the Facilitating Environment*. Hogarth Press, London

III

PERSON AND LOVE

The social background to the Judaeo–Christian teaching on fornication and adultery has been the lowly status of woman, the overwhelming importance of children and, in the Christian era, the hostility towards sexual pleasure. Gradually most societies are moving towards the position where their primary need is not to populate the world but to keep population under control, so that it does not exceed the world's food resources. At the same time as this basic change is occurring, women are seeking recognition of their equality of worth with men, and the almost universal androcentricity which has influenced so much of the background of moral thinking will have to take into account the needs and rights of women as they emerge from simply being objects suitable for procreation and merely meeting men's sexual appetites. These social changes will inevitably draw attention to the next layer of psychological values, that is to say to those criteria which define the essentials of being a person which in fact means a sexual person, who enters into a relationship of equality and complementarity with another to realise the meaning of love.

Person

Defining the criteria of being a person is an immense and complex task. First, there is the need to agree on the inherent characteristics which together constitute a person. Secondly, a person is placed in a particular social environment and the social values prevailing in that society contribute to the particular definition of person. Thirdly, there is the spiritual dimension which reflects spiritual values with or without a God-faith dimension.

In this chapter, however, we can seek our definition in Western society with its Judaeo–Christian tradition while remaining mindful of the dangers in attempting to provide universals for 'natural law' principles which neglect social variables. In our narrow definition we can concentrate on the fact that a person is a psychosomatic unity who, from the time of conception onwards, realises his/her physical, intellectual, psychological (affective and cognitive perspectives) and spiritual dimensions within the particular socio-economic matrix of his/her society. The psychological key to being a person is the dynamic concept of *wholeness*, that is to say, having access in a balanced form to all one's dimensions, both conscious and unconscious, and *growth*, a continuous process which allows the realisation of one's potential. The essentials of person are therefore the constituents of psychosomatic unity, their integration into a dynamic whole and the growth of the summated potential of the whole.

Thus here is a moral dimension which is no longer concerned with parts of a person, for example, the negative characteristic of avoiding the act of fornication, but with a constant positive pursuit of remaining and growing as a person. All human activity, both intra- and inter-personal, is now seen in terms of enhancing or diminishing the potential of being fully human. If this principle is accepted, certain moral consequences follow.

Wholeness and Growth

One essential moral consequence is to be found in the concept that all human behaviour needs to attempt to engage the *whole* person. When men or women deliberately set out to experience one dimension of their being alone i.e. physical, intellectual or psychological, then there is a diminution of the image of God in man. Thus when behaviour concentrates exclusively on the sexual or the use of reason at the expense of the body or feelings, or on feelings at the expense of the body or the mind, there is the danger of the dehumanisation, fragmentation and diminution of being a person. Secondly, when intra- or inter-personal behaviour is occurring, it is necessary not only to recognise and accept affirmatively the fullness of one's being (this is what love of self means) but also to aim to achieve those conditions in life which foster integrated growth, the realisation of one's potential which is summed up in Christ's injunction to be as perfect as our heavenly Father. Whatever else perfection may involve, in psychological terms it means wholeness and growth – dynamic terms which imply righteousness in its various aspects.

Thus, as far as sexual behaviour is concerned, the new framework of moral reference will primarily have little to do with sexual pleasure *per se* but will be concerned with the moral requirement of authenticating the person in ourselves and in our neighbours. From this it follows that any behaviour that merely concentrates on the sexual reduces the potential of being fully human and that moral criteria will be found in the missing intellectual and psychological dimensions; that is to say, the morality of fornication is essentially a morality of the missing personal elements which are not engaged in the interaction. But if the whole person is engaged, how can we define the fullest realisation of human potential in the interaction? The Christian answer is in the presence of love. But how is love to be defined in such interaction?

The Essentials of Personal Love

In my various writings[1] I have tried to specify the meaning of love by using three key words, sustaining, healing and growth, which in turn demand certain contingencies of permanency, continuity and predictability. Here I will simply mention them briefly.

Sustaining

We enter into this world in a one to one relationship between ourselves and our mother and this one to one bond or attachment remains fundamental to all our subsequent human experience. The first element of such experience is that of sustaining. We cannot survive our early years unless someone, usually our mother, provides us with material sustenance. The need to be provided for materially continues throughout life whenever our own ability to look after ourselves is temporarily or permanently impaired. With the rapid social changes affecting the status of women, their traditional economic dependence on men is diminishing and so is the need to please and placate through fear of economic damage. But there is of course more to sustaining than material welfare although clearly this comes first. There is emotional sustaining which basically means security. Security in turn means that we need to have meaning, recognition, acceptance and significance for another person who is in touch with our inner world through sensitive, empathetic communication and reacts to our needs with increasing accuracy. Reacting sensitively to our material and emotional sustaining needs does not mean necessarily eliminating them or providing all the answers. It does require however a minimum degree of permanency, continuity and predictability to allay our fears of abandonment, loss, repudiation and rejection.

Healing

Beyond sustaining we reach a deeper layer of our being. If we feel sufficiently sustained, we show consciously or unconsciously to the person who is showing evidence of love the wounds we have accumulated up to that moment of time. These wounds are clamouring for healing; they are the wounds we have brought into the world through our genetic and constitutional make-up, and the wounds we have sustained in the course of our upbringing. Healing such personal wounds is a particular responsibility of the psychological

38

sciences. It is the psychiatrist or the psychologist in special cases who will treat disorders of thought, mood, anxiety, the ability to relate at all or in a non-destructive manner which involves the familiar problems of excessive aggression, jealousy, envy and so on, but healing is not a prerogative of the behavioural sciences. We can all act as agents of healing by giving each other new healing experiences, providing the missing elements of security, trust, encouragement or whatever is needed and removing the threats of insecurity, deprivation etc. The great discovery of Freud through psychoanalysis was that the therapist can provide a second chance in life, a second opportunity to correct some of the experiences that went wrong the first time round in our childhood. Provided there is a relationship of love in and through sustaining, we can reach a bit further and deeper and become agents of healing towards each other. It hardly needs saying that healing cannot easily occur under circumstances of transient relationships. If we are going to take the risk of exposing our painful wounds, we need to trust the other sufficiently to feel that he or she can take our pain and handle it with care and effectiveness. This needs time, continuity, reliability and predictability. The essentials of healing do not occur in transient relationships although something good and precious can be bestowed in a transient relationship. But there is a world of difference between experiencing *something* good and entering into a relationship which gradually transforms our deepest wounds, healing the whole person.

Growth

Without the presence of sustaining or healing, personal growth faces enormous difficulties. Briefly, when we refer to growth we mean the obvious physical, intellectual or social growth that characterises the first two decades of life. This is self evident, but there is also the far harder concept of psychological maturation, achieving wholeness which plays such an important role in Jungian psychology. This growth means the transformation of physical prowess to athletic excellence,

39

of intelligence to wisdom, of feelings and emotions to sensitive awareness and generous empathetic response. In brief, growth implies availability and realisation of potential. Availability means physical, psychological and intellectual access to oneself in an affirmative manner and hence to others. It is another expression of the dictum of loving one's neighbour as oneself.

It is essential to note that for growth we need not only ourselves but others because growth occurs in relationships. The most advantageous growth occurs within relationships which are not overwhelmed either by the need for survival, that is to say sustaining has been met minimally, or in which our wounds are not so obtrusive that most of our energy is taken up in coping with the attendant problems. Once again the most conducive conditions for growth are relationships of permanency, continuity, reliability and predictability which allow the partners to understand one another and to act as facilitating agents, bringing to the fore the other's hidden talents and helping to formulate clearly that which is latent and confused within; each acting, in other words, as midwives to the other by rendering conscious the unconscious, confirming talent in place of doubt and uncertainty, reinforcing initiative, encouraging experimentation, providing succour at times of pain, failure and despair, helping us to face and integrate the dark side of ourselves.

This is not to say that we cannot learn things from others or they from us in transient relationships but it does mean that the more enduring and widespread growth occurs within relationships that allow a reciprocal revelation of the widest possible range of our inner world.

Marriage as a Permanent Relationship

Let us forget for a moment all that we were brought up to understand by marriage, namely that it is a relationship between a man and a woman for the purpose of procreation and education of children carrying with it the implicit conditions of faithfulness and permanency, and let us look at it in an entire-

40

ly different manner. Let us see it as *the* relationship which, through its commitment to permanency, continuity, reliability, and predictability, offers the most common human conditions for the promotion of love in terms of sustaining, healing and growth. Then we have an alternative moral framework in which to place fornication and adultery. Neither of them are seen now in terms of illicit sexual acts of pleasure but as threats to those conditions which are the best enablers for the provision of love.

If this formulation is accepted, then we can see that the morality of pre-marital sexual intercourse has nothing to do primarily with sexual pleasure but with the best provisions for the promotion of the life of the couple. It is for this reason that I would still maintain that a commitment of permanency, which carries implicitly the attempt at continuity, predictability and reliability for the purposes of sustaining, healing and growth, is the most appropriate condition for defining the starting point of married life.

Should such a moment be a public occasion? Clearly the public occasion cannot by itself furnish the internal motivation of love which the couple bring to each other but it can reinforce it by involving the community as a public witness, to externalise what was hitherto internal. The wedding ceremony must, however, be more than an empty symbol. It should be a reciprocal acknowledgement by both the couple and society of their newly formed social, legal, emotional and physical relationship, laying down boundaries between the couple and others but at the same time opening channels of needs, establishing social networks of friendship and creating new possibilities of human interaction. All too often the married couple are left to their own devices after the wedding when this is the time they need a great deal of non-interfering but genuine support. The realities of the late Middle Ages with the problems of clandestine marriages still apply in our age. Relationships are never exclusively personal, they have a social context and a permanent relationship has perhaps more social significance than any other.

By now some readers will be screaming what about the children? Is not this what marriage is all about? The answer is

41

yes and no. No, marriage is not exclusively about children and the Church has always accepted this by accepting the sterile marriage and the marriage that occurs after the menopause. First and foremost, marriage is a relationship of life and love between a man and a woman, based on mutual donation of selves. But, of course, Yes, marriage is about new life, about children but these cannot prosper if the life of their parents is not stable and loving.

The implicit link between coitus, pleasure and procreation which has dominated Christian thinking has to give way to person, relationship, life and love in which the pre-eminence given to the life of the children follows and does not precede the life of the spouses. Marriage is first of all a community of love between a husband and wife, and only afterwards a family. In an entirely new sexual morality the accent is first and foremost on the relationship of the couple at all stages of its development, for this is the best preparation for the life of the children.

NOTES

1. (a) Dominian J. 1975 *Cycles of Affirmation*. Darton, Longman and Todd, London.
   (b) Dominian J. and Peacocke A. R. 1976 *From Cosmos to Love*. Darton, Longman and Todd, London.

IV

ADOLESCENT MASTURBATION

GENERAL MORAL PRINCIPLES

Within the current framework of sexual morality masturbation has been a simple issue for the moralist. Here par excellence was sexual pleasure separated first from intercourse, secondly from intercourse within marriage, and thirdly from the possibility of being directed towards a new life. On all these scores it has been repeatedly defined as intrinsically evil. Recently a discussion was printed in the Clergy Review[1] in which the opinion of eminent theologians was that a distinction has to be made between pastoral theology, that is to say the responsibility of the priest in the course of assessing every day behaviour and events, and the objective morality of such behaviour and events according to permanent and unchanging moral principles based on natural law. Certainly the priest who has to advise his flock needs to take a very different attitude from the cold objectivity of moral principles, hence in the matter of masturbation, as in other areas of sexual ethics, the rigour of moral objectivity has been transformed by the existential reality of knowledge, understanding, freedom of action, intention etc. Those brought up in the traditional moral theology know by heart the criteria for sin, namely the presence of evil matter, full knowledge and full consent, and, depending on the gravity of the subject matter, a distinction was made between mortal and venial sin. Using such criteria or modifications thereof, masturbation had of late been treated increasingly lightly, just as contraception was beginning to be handled prior to Humanae Vitae. The recent Declaration on Sexual Ethics brought the same sharp reminder to the Church that no such liberties can be taken with traditional morality in the matter of masturbation. But just as in the issue of contraception, there are all sorts of mitigating pastoral reasons, so once again equivalent pastoral reasons will be found to circumvent the rigour of this pronouncement. I must make my own position clear here. This seems to me to be utterly dishonest. Either the moral teaching is the correct one and the whole Church must be summoned to find the moral courage to obey it, or else the endless finding of mitigating reasons is simply an escape for a confused community of pastors and Christians who are trying to do their best in difficult circumstances. But in these circumstances, when a large part of the Church is trying to circumvent the implications of its official teaching, it should not be surprised if the rest of the Christian community and society as a whole cannot take too seriously the importance of the pronouncements on contraception or masturbation. Either the official teaching is right and reasonably clear enough to command universal or nearly so acceptance or it is not, in which case the sooner the Church as a whole moves on to the next stage the better. It is my personal view that the Church is *not* right in its attitude to masturbation and the rest of this chapter will attempt to state the reasons.

Morality based on Person

It is abundantly clear that the prohibition of masturbation is a carry-over from the negative attitude to sexual pleasure and the denial of its ultimate legitimate outlet in a biological potentiality of procreative mutual giving within marriage. Now this is a morality based on the claims of biology without examining or doing full justice to the claims of the growth of the human personality. Here as elsewhere in my writings, the

44

insistence has been that the only legitimate moral basis for assessing sexual behaviour is its appropriateness to persons in their wholeness. Masturbation must be placed in the context of what is happening to a young man or woman over a period of a few years between puberty and the time when they can have a full personal relationship with another person, usually of the opposite sex. Until the advent of heterosexual friendship, there is a period of transition in which puberty, with all its consequences, invades the whole person, body, mind, feelings, and has certain results.

Separation between Child and Parent

The crucial characteristic of personal growth in the first two decades of life is a gradual separation between child and parent, so that, by the end of the second decade, adolescents are ready to assume an independent existence, that is to say, to possess and control sufficiently their bodies, minds and feelings so as to be able to assume full responsibility for a separate life. The work of Piaget[2] has given us a broad outline of the way cognitive autonomy is assumed, the work of the various psychoanalytical schools have given us an outline of how emotional autonomy is reached and there is an extensive anatomical and physiological knowledge to give us the most detailed information on how the body reaches the peak of its biological development.

Puberty and Incest

Puberty is an event which overlaps both the physical and the psychological categories of personal growth. Everyone knows the biological characteristics. For the girl, this is the time of internal and external physiological changes leading to breast enlargement, ovulation, monthly periods and therefore the beginning of the possibility of fertilisation. For the boy, analogous hormonal changes occur leading to the secondary sexual characteristics of change of voice, the growth of facial hair, the enlargement of the testicles and penis, the production of spermatozoa and the advent of spontaneous emissions and of masturbation. It should be remembered that some boys can in fact have an erection long before puberty but usually all these physiological and psychological events coincide. Traditional morality, which of course has its roots in ages when marriage and childbearing occurred earlier than nowadays, was entirely preoccupied with the social and physiological consequences of these changes and above all the biological possibility of starting a new life. As our advances in knowledge proceed, we realise more than ever that the well being of a new life depends utterly on the stability and well being of the parents and therefore it is the adult's progress towards maturity that must assume the supreme moral value. What is happening to the adolescent in his or her advance towards a mature, autonomous existence, enabling them to be stable and loving parents, now becomes the principal human issue which dictates the morality of personal events.

One of the main consequences of puberty is to place an incest barrier between child and parent, a most powerful separating force in the process of gradual autonomy. The incest barrier coincides with other intellectual and emotional separating processes, but this sexual separation places an absolute space between the two and gives the child the most significant facilitating opportunity to realise that it is *he* or *she* who possess their own body. Their body no longer belongs to father or mother; it is their own in all aspects, including now its sexual potentiality. The ability to realise, accept, handle and control this new dimension is a vital aspect of personal growth during puberty and adolescence.

Puberty and Aloneness

One of the most powerful psychological consequences of this inevitable step forward in personal growth is an internal isolation, aloneness and possibly loneliness. It is a period in our lives when our bodies are invaded by powerful hormones with the most pronounced external physical changes and a psychological and emotional confusion of not knowing how to form our immediate bonds of friendship and attachment. We have to move away from our parents and we are not ready to belong exclusively to anybody else because we do not know who and what we are. A time interval is required to experience our body with its new characteristics, to find out our capacity to form relationships with our peers and this discovery of ourself needs time, experience and, inevitably, experimentation

Psychiatrists in fact see in the course of their work the young men and women who cannot find themselves adequately or effectively. These are the adolescents who cling to their home and parents because they are afraid to face their independence, or who go 'off the rails' by an exaggerated response of independence, sexual experimentation, rebellion, repudiation of work or study. These youngsters have often been called drop outs or relegated to the bottom of the permissive league of our age. When they do not have to face the familiar condemnations and judgements of parents, teachers and relations, they often sit quietly, parading their utter despair, with their isolation and loneliness in full view, challenging one to give them a reason for living. They do not wish to turn back and form a relationship of dependence with their parents, they cannot go forward because of their fears and anxieties and form a relationship of equality with their peers. They are stranded in no man's land and their despair is often turned into suicidal gestures, excessive drinking, drug taking or total abandonment of responsibility. Technically this state has been called an identity crisis of adolescence. These are the men and women who experiment freely with their bodies but do not feel they possess them, in fact the apparent excessive sexual indulgence is often a seeking of emotional or sexual reassurance that they possess anything worthwhile at all. Under the guise of adulthood, they are frightened children not knowing who they are or with whom they can form a relationship of love.

If we adopt an entirely different framework of reference, namely that of love and person, we can see immediately that puberty and masturbation are linked intimately as one process of personal growth.

As far as love is concerned, there is a constant need for the growing person to be familiar in an affirmative manner with the progressive changes in his/her body, mind and feelings. The transformed post pubertal body has to be experienced as having continuity with the past and the new self experienced as something good. The invasion of the body by sexual hormones involves the possibility of genital sexual arousal. To experience this fully and consciously, with all the attendant sexual pleasure, is no more than an acknowledgement of the changes which the Creator has designed as appropriate for this phase of personal development. One way of exploring and accepting a separate sexual identity is through masturbation for in this way the new dimensions of the body are discovered and their intrinsic goodness acknowledged and incorporated in the emerging personality. The pubertal body is not primarily designed for procreative purposes. It is a stage of identity growth which prepares the way for adult personal relationships. To bring forward the application of a sexual morality of marriage to puberty is a notion which has no possible justification.

Beyond the need to learn to accept positively the emerging pubertal sexual transformation, masturbation is a limited but genuine comfort for the inner loneliness and isolation of this period of life. It is also a transition phenomenon leading to full sexual activity which is other-person orientated. But time is needed to bring order out of the confusion of adolescence, to discover who one is and what he/she has to offer to another person. This too is learned by trial and error and through the social mores of the particular society.

Masturbation needs to be seen as a transition phenomenon which serves to acquaint the individual with the newly acquired sexual dimensions of the body, giving them an affirmative and positive experience of these, providing temporary comfort in the crisis of personal identification and leading the way to personal relationships which are overwhelmingly heterosexual. The evidence that we possess also suggests that masturbation abates in frequency as adult sexual relationships replace this solitary experience and only returns in circumstances of forced or pathological social or psychological isolation.

The Dangers of Masturbation

The concern over masturbation has not been confined to Christian circles. Others with no particular religious orientation have written with great flourish about its dangers. Every possible pathology from mental insanity to physical disorders have been attributed to masturbation.[3] Needless to say there is not the slightest evidence that it is responsible for any disease or disorder and these fears have been relegated to their proper place as historical curios, figments of man's infinite imagination to find explanations for the unknown. From time to time, I receive letters from various sources which remind me of the psychological dangers of masturbation, which is stated to be a dangerous habit, difficult to give up later on in life and inimical to satisfactory mature adult sexual relationships. There can be no doubt that there are adult men and women who, despite appearances to the contrary, are solitary people, unable to form close relationships with others, who resort, either occasionally or excessively, to masturbation. The mistake here is to confuse cause and effect. It is not the masturbation which acts as an inhibiting agent to adult intimate personal relationships but the failure of personal growth. Almost invariably closer examination of such men and women shows psychological traumatic events which have acted as inhibiting factors either in their ability to form close personal or satisfactory sexual relationships. In fact there is no evidence whatsoever that masturbation has any adverse physical or emotional impact in its transitional pubertal adolescent phase.

To summarise, there is need for a totally new conceptualisation of the morality of masturbation, now seen primarily as an intrinsic component of personal growth during puberty and adolescence, with its own distinctive phase morality, which in no way justifies the anticipation of principles governing sexual activity at any later stage in human development.

NOTES

1. The Clergy Review, June 1976. The Declaration on Certain Questions concerning Sexual Ethics.
2. Maier H. W. 1969 *Three Theories of Child Development*. Harper International Edition, New York.
3. Hare E. H. 1962 Masturbation Insanity, The History of an Idea. Journal of Mental Science 108, 1.

V

PRE-MARITAL SEX

The weakness of using the presence of sexual pleasure and openness to biological life as the common moral denominator for judging the legitimacy of any particular sexual conduct is most clearly evident in the moral issue of sexual activity which progresses from masturbation, which is intra-personal to sexual intercourse which is an interpersonal event. Throughout this book the emphasis is that the basis of a new sexual morality must be founded on the concept of person and love. Masturbation does not involve any other human being whereas the pleasure of sexual intercourse does involve another human being and so entirely different considerations prevail. Let us remind ourselves for a moment of the traditional reasons for condemning premarital intercourse.

As far as theology is concerned, there is clearly the teaching that sexual intercourse is legitimate only within marriage with a procreative potential present. In this area of behaviour, the Augustinian teaching could be re-inforced by scriptural texts which forbade fornication ('But the body – this is not meant for fornication; it is for the Lord.' I Cor. 6,13.) and so the religious foundation for such opposition had a much stronger case. Apart from scriptural revelation, there was in addition a wide range of natural hazards, the loss of virginity where this was prized socially, the fear of pregnancy, venereal disease and, in dire circumstances abortion, all of which provided a second line of powerful argumentation against such behaviour.

But over the last few decades, powerful voices have been raised from both non-Christian and Christian sources which have questioned the legitimacy of all these warnings and prohibitions. Let us consider these criticisms one by one. The advent of contraceptives is said to have eliminated the danger of pregnancy. This is of course both true and false. It is true that properly taken precautions eliminate the risk of becoming pregnant. But these precautions are not always taken, nor do they always work, otherwise there would be no need for abortions, which still feature in tens of thousands, by no means all of these involve married couples. Certain contraceptive precautions mitigate against venereal disease but certainly these diseases have not been eradicated and there have been in fact waves of recrudescence in recent times which remind us of this constant danger. There are of course those who maintain that a V.D. infection is not a serious matter and that too much fuss is made of these conditions. Very few will follow this line of thought, but many more will argue that fear is not a good basis for love or morality and all these arguments are based primarily on fear. As far as Christianity is concerned, it is a faith based on love, not fear, and certainly cannot use the latter as its main argument. I would dispute, however, that all these are primarily arguments based on fear. They are arguments based on personal responsibility for the well-being of another person and oneself. Even those who believe abortion is morally legitimate (which incidentally I do not) must accept that to face a woman with the necessity for this action is neither responsible nor loving.

There are, however, further arguments from Christian sources which have to be considered. Perhaps the most powerful one expressed by young people is the fact that a wedding ceremony adds nothing to the personal love felt by two people. Indeed they have seen too many so-called 'proper' Christian marriages end in disaster to be convinced that the key of love is to be found in a ceremony, however symbolic and beautiful it may be. This is a powerful criticism and, as we shall see later on in this chapter, has some strength from tradition, but

52

it portrays an appalling theological ignorance. The whole teaching of the Church that marriage begins with the consent of reciprocal giving of self consummated by the first act of sexual intercourse is a bit of information which most young people listen to with amazement and, having done so, are more convinced than ever of the folly of the Christian tradition which puts so much emphasis on a ceremony and one act of consummation, when they know that marriage is a relationship spanning many decades which begins after the wedding ceremony. If at this point, one tries to introduce the major changes found in Vatican II which indicate that the Church is moving in this direction, there is usually a sigh of restless confusion. So much for our teaching on this vital sacrament! However, when all is said and done, we still have to convince them that a public ceremony is one of the essential components of this sacrament and that somehow this ceremony is linked in an essential manner with love.

More sophisticated Christian arguments opposing fornication as immoral suggest that women were no more than chattels in the Old Testament and therefore fornication was therefore a matter of property rights. Whatever partial truth there may be in such an exegetical approach, it does not provide an adequate basis for the condemnation of fornication which in its very essence is concerned with personal relationships of responsibility, attachment, faithfulness and therefore ultimately of love.

I believe that the crucial question regarding pre-marital sexual intercourse concerns the fact that post-pubertally men and women are capable of genital union within a whole range of personal relationship from no commitment whatsoever, the essence of prostitution, to that of a permanent life-long commitment, the essence of marriage. Christianity has hitherto simplified this complexity with an absolute ban on pre-marital sexual intercourse, and certainly from the point of view of an objective morality this has great advantages: every sexual act before marriage is wrong, every sexual act after marriage is at least legitimate within it. But immediately will come back the predictable comment that a great deal of sexuality within marriage is *not* an expression of love, whereas love can be present before marriage. Thus it is essential to examine what we mean by love and attempt to define three common differing patterns of pre-marital sexual intercourse. Chapter III was devoted to answering in outline what is meant by love. What follows are three easily recognisable patterns of pre-marital sexual activity which need to be distinguished. They are characterised by greater or lesser involvement, commitment to and responsibility for the other person which are the essential features of love.

Promiscuous behaviour

Promiscuous behaviour is characterised by the total repudiation of any exclusive involvement, commitment or responsibility for the other and it is essentially what has been understood for centuries by the concept of prostitution. Here is an encounter of bodies with or without a contractual pay obligation. Traditionally, the prostitute has been the woman who is prepared, for a fee, to make her body available to a man. There are of course male prostitutes as well, the gender of the person is immaterial. The fact is that the exchange is contained in the realisation of sexual pleasure alone, without any attendant personal relationship. Those who claim that sexual pleasure has its own justification, and the more the merrier, would find such behaviour legitimate and acceptable. And indeed there are those who participate in such transient once-only coitus whenever the opportunity allows. Nowadays such conduct is not necessarily confined to intercourse with prostitutes because there are seriously proposed views that sexual pleasure should be entirely separated from love in personal relationships. Christianity is particularly weak in answering this claim when it proposes a sexual morality based primarily on biological-physiological principles, for this is precisely the justification for this behaviour: sexual intercourse is treated as a physical event leading to pleasure and carrying its own physiological procreative justification. Clearly such an explanation is grossly insufficient, but a different value system is needed to answer satisfactorily the claim of utter hedonism. What is needed is the value system of love which *conceives human relationships as involving the interaction of whole persons encountering mind, body and feelings in each other. When mind and feelings and particularly the latter are ignored there is a diminution of the wholeness of both partners and therefore an inevitable dehumanization in the exchange.*

This is not to say that there are not some people who are so seriously wounded in their personality that they can only tolerate such partial exchange. Any further involvement is beyond their capacity. Only the most intimate knowledge of the inner world of such people can give us the insight necessary to understand their personal limitations. Nevertheless a distinction has to be made between recognition of such human limitations of psychological potential and the advancement of promiscuity as an acceptable ideology on the grounds that sexual intercourse is a physiological event which provides release of sexual tension, pleasure and comfort and needs no further justification. But the reply surely must be that what is clearly needed is the involvement of more than bodies if the exchange is to be justifiably called human.

Transient Relationships

Next in the order of premarital behaviour comes precisely those exchanges which are more than casual, single exchanges. Here sexual intercourse takes place after two people get to know each other and have a much greater access to each other's feelings and minds. Sexual intercourse now becomes an expression of friendship which, however, is still conducted on the acknowledged basis of transience. Whether the friendship lasts for days, weeks or months, or even intermittently over a period of years, there is no commitment to exclusiveness and permanency, and certainly not to having children and raising a family.

It will be seen at once that a different order of human encounter is now present. There is nothing casual about such an exchange and those who accept it bring to each other many tokens of the interaction which could be described as love. The two prominent features in this exchange are the absence of any permanent commitment and the deliberate refusal to have children. The refusal to have children is important but not crucial, in the sense that the Church recognises the sterile marriage. Nevertheless all transient sexual relationships prior to marriage would be described as fornication. So what are the objections to it?

As already mentioned, there is always the risk that a child will be conceived which may require an abortion or adoption. The problems of illegitimacy may lead to unpleasant discoveries for the child later on in life, and finally there is the possibility of being brought up by a single parent with all its attendant difficulties. No one can dismiss any of these possibilities as inconsequential. But if a child is not conceived, is there a core of fundamental objection to this pattern of behaviour?

It seems to me that it is of the very essence of human attachment, and therefore of love, to wish to experience continuity with a person who has aroused genuine feelings, by reaching, in however limited a manner, the whole of ourselves. In all such relationships fear of loss and therefore jealousy must inevitably creep in. For once a person has involved the whole of our being, it is natural to wish to continue that relationship and commitment means continuity, reliability, predictability and responsibility for each other. Relationships are placed under great strain when they have to live under the shadow of unilateral repudiation without any recourse or appeal to the contrary principle of continuity.

Many young people will take up precisely this point and claim that the commitment of permanency to marriage is not an expression of love but of bondage and that love only truly exists when there is absolute freedom. This argument has an element of truth in it, in the sense that love is at its best when it exceeds the bounds of mere duty, but everyone knows that such an appeal has also a powerful rationalisation behind it. There is a world of difference between the freedom of falling in love and loving, and the latter needs constant effort and renewal which can only be truly achieved within a framework of dependable and predictable commitment. Transient relationships condemn couples to permanent uncertainty about their future. It is true that marriage is no guarantee of progressive and uninterrupted growth of love, but it does contain an essential commitment to a sustained effort to overcome the obstacles which prevent the growth of love by providing a framework of security which is so necessary for the sustenance and growth of love.

Trial Marriages

Many couples will acknowledge all the above objectives and in fact avoid sexual intercourse until they have reached an explicit understanding that they wish to live together in an exclusive commitment, as a form of trial marriage. Implicit in such a relationship is a conditional clause. If the relationship works out, it may be followed by a public ceremony. This is a variant of the transient relationship, with a much greater commitment which just falls short of the permanency of marriage and which still excludes children. The words 'trial marriage' are of course a social and psychological contradiction. The essence of marriage is the full and exclusive availability of self in a commitment of permanency and there is no such thing as a trial marriage. Permanency is an essential feature of marriage, even in the presence of divorce, for it expresses one of the most profound human psychological needs and objectives; namely to remain united permanently with the source of love which completes and complements us. Thus the same objections apply to trial marriages as to transient relationships.

Permanent Relationship without a Marriage Ceremony

We finally reach the couple who have made the implicit and explicit commitment to a permanent relationship and to children but who refuse to postpone a full sexual life prior to a marriage ceremony. Officially, of course, they are going against the teaching of the Church, but tradition is not entirely against them. There was a period in the history of the

Church in which the constitutive factor of marriage lay, not in the benediction, but in the mutual consent of the partners, who were able to commit themselves fully to each other, consummate their union sexually and, in the eyes of the Church, were considered validly married without a wedding ceremony. The difficulties arising from this situation of private commitment was the increasing problem in which partners committed themselves fully to more than one person, and the scandal of clandestine marriages forced the Church ultimately to insist on a public ceremony, in the presence of the parish priest and two witnesses. Thus the wedding ceremony, although historically very old, has its specfic origin through the social problems of the late Middle Ages. But the essential Christian teaching has been that the sacrament of marriage is the freely given, exclusive mutual donation of two persons, a man and woman, who offer the whole of self, mind, body and feelings, to each other in a permanent relationship which naturally has new life as one of its principal objectives but a sterile couple have always been considered no less truly married. The validity of marriage does not depend on the couple's fertility but on their mutually exclusive consenting availability which is first and foremost the source of life for each other and subsequently the origin of new life.

It will be seen at once that by any criterion the traditional view of fornication, which has focused on a single sexual act prior to marriage, cannot remotely do justice to the innumerable different circumstances in which the act or acts occur prior to marriage. What really matters is the encounter of persons and the presence of love. The fact that a great variety of sexual activity prior to marriage is classed together is itself a profound reason for reassessing the moral categories of fornication and its meaning.

VI

SEX IN MARRIAGE

The crisis in sexual morality has arisen for various reasons. Some of these reflect profound changes in human conditions, others transient historical phenomena. Thus the reaction against Victorian prudery may well be followed by a backlash of puritanism. Such swings of social mores are not unknown. The temporary weakness of religion as a moral force may also be followed by a totally different climate. What will not change in time, indeed will increase in pace and understanding, is man's control over fertilisation. This is a profound social and biological change. As men and women learn to control fertilisation with increasing accuracy, we shall virtually reach a stage where a new life will be created by one act of intercourse or at the very most a few more. Such absolute control over the moment of fertilisation is even more important in the long run than population control. There may well be advances in food production which will change the population resources of this globe. There may be catastrophes which will necessitate extensive re-population. Whatever the future of population may hold, one fact is certain: control over the moment of fertilisation will mean that the quantitive link between sexual intercourse and new life is being severed, in that 99 per cent of sexual activity will be knowingly non-reproductive in the future. This is already affecting millions of people and will become a universal patterning in a predictable period of time. This is the most fundamental reason why Christianity must find a totally different basis for its theology of sexuality from its primary link with new life which will slowly become subordinate to something which must by definition be far more inclusive. There is a good deal of hesitation in Christian circles when it comes to finding the courage to give an alternative meaning to sexuality with absolute certainty that it reflects the image of God in man. One must say at once that such an alternative exists, has always existed, and simply implies understanding sex as being at the service of life, first the life of the couple and then, through the life of the couple, initiating first the biological but infinitely more important, sustaining the psychological, social and spiritual life of the children, their life being seen now in terms of quality and not quantity.

Sex and New Life

If sex is seen primarily as being at the service of the life of the couple spanning many decades of marital relationship, then the order of priorities of value are clearly social and psychological not biological. In the framework of the morality of sexuality proposed in this book, it is utterly unacceptable to place the supreme value of human sexuality at the biological point of fertilisation which engages only a part of the whole person, however significant that part is, and certainly it is totally in contradiction to the meaning of sexuality when we realise that at most the contribution of coitus to new life will be on a very few occasions. Hence to place the supreme value of human sexuality on its openness to biological life is unacceptable because it emphasises a part (however vital that part may be) and therefore intrinsically dehumanises the sexual encounter by its order of priorities. What every sexual act must attempt to do is to engage the *whole* person, body, mind and feelings; the emphasis on the *biological part* is an intrinsic diminution of the wholeness of the encounter, even the bodily encounter. Secondly, the biological fusion will occur so rarely that the centre of significance can no longer lie there. These and other objections against the insistence in Humanae Vitae on the openness of every sexual act to new life have been made by many authors. They are briefly repeated here to show that this particular element of the encyclical cannot be the basis for a new sexual morality. In all honesty it does not claim to offer anything new in this regard, even though other parts of it which refer to the Vatican II statement on marriage and the family contain fruitful notions. Equally, its insistence on the traditional view of the dangers of sexual pleasure makes it necessary to part company with the document on this matter also.

Sex at the service of a Permanent Relationship

In the previous chapter the need to reexamine and assess various categories of pre-marital sexual relationships was considered. Marriage has been described as a relationship of love which aims to foster sustaining, healing and growth and that these characteristics need continuity, reliability and predictability, in other words permanency. Within permanency, the couple attempt to reach the whole of each other as persons and to do so in a manner that serves their realisation of their potential, their movement towards perfection. Sexual intercourse must from now on increasingly be seen as having the primary purpose of serving this inter-personal wholeness and realisation of potential.

Sex as a Body Language

Everyone knows the essential features leading to sexual intercourse. There is first of all sexual attraction which leads to genital arousal and the consequent rise of emotional and bodily tension. This is further heightened by erotic foreplay, leading to genital union and to an orgasmic culmination of intense pleasure, a release of tension and a sense of immense closeness when both the participants are enjoying the act. Such is the instinctual intensity of the experience that most societies, and certainly Christian societies, have been bemused by it in their appraisal and value systems, and yet, when we come to consider the dangers that have been attributed to sexual intercourse, they largely centre on the fact that this intense passion overwhelms men and women reducing their rational control in an impulsive frenzy. In this book this point is treated radically differently. Instead of concentrating on the dangers of the passion involved in sexual pleasure, the view is taken that such an intense experience should be harnessed in the interest of the inter-personal encounter, now no longer seen in terms of its procreative potential but in the service of love. Thus the movement in society to promote the value of sexual pleasure is right, but the limitations, and indeed the dangers, stem from the partial involvement of the whole person when the body only is engaged. There is nothing wrong with sexual pleasure, but it must be directed to serve the relationship as a whole. How does it do that? Happily married couples know this intuitively even though they cannot describe it in so many words. Sexual intercourse becomes the silent body language that serves the following purposes:

Gratitude

Sexual intercourse is the recurrent language of thanksgiving. It is the way that two people say to each other 'Thank you for today, for yesterday, for the day before, for the months, years we have struggled to reach this point'.

Hope

It is the language of hope. The intense pleasure and closeness of intercourse renew regularly the basis of the relationship. With or without words, a couple are saying to each other in 'I hope you will be here tomorrow, and the day after and for many months and years until the end of our life together'.

Reconciliation

It is the language that can act as a powerful source of reconciliation. How many arguments and quarrels are resolved during successful love-making!

Sexual Identification

It is the bodily language through which the couple can affirm most clearly each other's specific sexual identity. Coitus is one of the clearest ways of confirming the fact that a man is a man and a woman is a woman. It is a recurrent powerful source of sexual identification.

Acceptance and Equality

When a couple freely donate themselves in sexual intercourse in the absence of fear or coercion, this is an act which exemplifies fully mutual equality and acceptance. This is where woman's increasing emancipation means that she is likely to be involved sexually in a freely willed reciprocal activity and not as the object for the man's fulfilment or out of fear that refusal will have adverse repercussions on her position. Rather coitus has the recurrent potential of affirming that husband and wife are the most precious persons in each other's life. Thus sexual intercourse serves most purposefully as a recurrent source which supplies the strength which fuels the sustaining, healing and growth of the couple, by its uniting potential.

Children

Whereas a few acts will be responsible for actual new life, every act has the potential of mobilising that love between the spouses which in turn serves the life of the children and provides them with a living model of love for their own life afterwards.

If sex is thus seen primarily as a life-giving source in terms of the relationship of the couple, there is no intrinsic reason for the avoidance either of contraception or of direct sterilisation. This is not to say that there are no moral issues appertaining to both. As far as contraception is concerned, the emphasis shifts from the recurrent openness to life to the nature of the contraceptive method which does not damage the oneness of the couple and so, as I have repeatedly stated, the Roman Catholic Church has a valid point against contraception but its case is based on the wrong grounds. The morality of contraception has nothing to do with the openness of every sexual act to new life but it has a lot to do with the method which allows for physical safety, fullness of physical experience, mutual responsibility of the couple. Similarly, sterilisation means that a part of the bodily component is no longer available for interaction and so the circumstances when sterilisation occurs should be judged very carefully. But if coitus is seen primarily as serving the relationship of the couple, provided a couple have the number of children they want, and if there are good reasons for it and sterilisation does not interfere with the fullness of the loving exchange, then within the moral framework of this book there is no basic moral reason to object to it.

Adultery and Fornication

Roman Catholic theologians, who have traditionally lumped together the morality of all sexual activity and condemned it as a whole outside marriage and in the absence of recurrent openness to life, will now be expecting the coup de grace whereby adultery and fornication will also be justified. But of course, just as with abortion, here are totally different moral categories.

An attempt has been made to describe sexual intercourse, the primary purpose of which is to foster love in a permanent relationship. The key moral issues are the description of love and the need for permanency and exclusiveness as those essential characteristics which foster and preserve love. Sexual intercourse can thus be seen either as a symbol for the realisation of pleasure alone or as a symbol which is primarily concerned with fostering love in a permanent relationship. Everything that I understand by the writings of the Old and New Testament emphasises the concepts of love and of relationship. The essence of the Judaeo–Christian faith is the relationship of faith and love between man/woman and God and between one human being and another. Fornication and adultery, unlike contraception and sterilisation (about which there is no clear cut reference in the Scriptures), are constantly mentioned in the Scriptures as evidence of the symbolic or real violation of relationship and love. Neither fornication nor adultery are best assessed in terms of single acts of sexual intercourse. Both are much better seen in the context of the relationship of love; in the case of fornication, whether a couple have reached the stage of creating a permanent relationship which can be served by sex; in the case of adultery whether there is a repudiation of the mutual faithfulness which the permanent relationship of love requires.

The Symbolic Value of Sexual Intercourse

We can summarise this chapter by stating that one expression for sexual intercourse in the Scriptures is the 'act of knowing' through which a couple come to relate to one another. The morality of sexual intercourse has thus been based on a knowledge which involves the whole person and which continues to be involved with the growing knowledge of the whole person with all the change and transformation which this involves over several decades. The real evil of our age is not the permissiveness of sexual pleasure but the impermanency of relationships whereby, through transience and divorce, human beings become stepping stones of temporary exploitation where the whole is never engaged and the depths are never touched. The responsibility of Christianity is not to be obsessed with the trivialisation of sex as a pleasure principle, but with the trivialisation of persons in the absence of genuine love which will be the theme of the next chapter.

VII

THE CRISIS OF LOVE

The attempts to rectify the current sexual problems in society by reasserting the traditional values and warning humanity against the dangers of illicit sexual pleasure are bound to fail, not so much because our age is specifically inclined towards self-destruction in this respect but because it faces a whole complex of circumstances which are completely new. At no time in the history of mankind have so many factors combined to influence sexual ethics.

The increasing control over fertilisation, combined with a reduction in family size, which has permeated throughout Western societies, has meant that the overwhelming majority of sexual activity no longer involves procreation. Sexual energy has been released in an unprecedented measure and has combined with other equally influential factors, such as: woman's pursuit of equality with men, so that the male's traditional sexual privileges are no longer his prerogative alone; increased psychological knowledge; Freudian principles transforming behavioural values. An enormous increase in material standards has laid the foundations and provided the security for the pursuit of alternative values.

It is the pursuit of these alternative values that divides society so intensely. The division extends beyond the demarcation of Christian and non-Christian values, although Christianity has a special role in sexual matters because the sexual ethics of Western society have been so powerfully shaped by Christian values and standards. The fact is that Western societies and gradually the whole of the world have to face afresh the purpose and meaning of the newly released sexual energy. I have never been satisfied with simply attacking our society as permissive, hedonistic or materialistic. This is an orthodox and traditional moral weapon of trying to influence human behaviour by attacking its proclivity towards gratification, whether it is sexual or material in nature. Such an approach can always have a limited success by mobilising guilt, but the remedy and the response need to be far more powerful than that associated with this sort of fervour.

In fact Western society must learn to handle both its material affluence and its new sexual freedom. The question remains how to incorporate both in value systems that respect man's authentic being and reflect Christian values. The answers are not far to seek.

At the most natural level, man's realisation of potential must ultimately serve the whole of his being, and therefore to remain attached primarily or solely at a material level is to neglect the potential of mind (intellect) and psyche (cognitive and affective). Western society has to find new values which do not fixate its citizens at the material level, and that means finding a place for the new and deeper layers of our humanity in terms of personal and inter-personal involvement. Traditionally this has meant turning towards a spiritual dimension, in fact towards God. This simple turning towards God will not in fact suffice. Man's involvement with God must take place at a level of engagement of the mind and psyche which is appropriate for a society that has immense opportunities of unravelling deeper layers of the image of God in man. That is why simplistic religious crusades just do not work. Man's spiritual longing is as strong as ever, but the level of engagement between man and God must reflect the realisation of these new depths in our humanity which the social, psychological and scientific horizons have opened up. One aspect of the spiritual crisis of the age is the inability of the churches to engage man accurately at a deeper level of existential experience which will do justice to these newly opened horizons. And yet the Christian answer is clearly there.

Christianity, through its teaching on poverty, has always shown mankind that although material things are precious, man does not live by bread (or the equivalent in our century) alone. Man lives by fullfilling his inner resources and what we must accept is the fact that there is a limit of what justice we can do to our humanity by pursuing one dimension alone, namely the material/physical. But we cannot pursue the spiritual either unless we acknowledge the new insights we have acquired in the depths of our psyche regarding our humanity.

This is the principle that must guide our approach to our newly discovered sexual resources. In order to go beyond hedonism, we must cease to exalt one dimension of being human, namely the realisation of sexual pleasure. Now this is where Christianity has a lot of work to do. First it must stop providing an excuse for hedonism. In most current writing on the pursuit of sexual pleasure, there is always some reference to the need to vindicate the human rights to sexual pleasure, so long denied by the negativity and hostility of Christian teaching. Without meaning to, Christianity has provided a useful excuse for the perpetuation of hedonism!

Having acknowledged the rightful place of sexual pleasure, the Christian response must shift from stressing sexual pleasure alone to human relationship. *At the very heart of hedonism is not the pursuit of sexual pleasure but the impermanency of human attachment.* We use others for our pleasure and neglect our responsibility to them as whole people. We collude with others to give us sexual pleasure at the expense of respecting the wholeness and depth of our own being. The traditional values implicit in the definition of fornication, adultery and divorce as evil were precisely the attempt to involve whole persons and the resistance to shallow, superficial, transient and incomplete human encounters. I repeat here a point made in the previous chapter. The evil of our age is not sexual permissiveness so much as the trivialisation of human encounter which, in the name of freedom, encourages the minimum engagement with the maximum haste and the maximum disengagement, as in pre-marital experimentation and divorce, with the minimum of effort in the presence of personal difficulties. The crisis of love lies in the fleeing from one human being to another in an attempt to find wholeness and fulfilment instead of engaging fully and overcoming the obstacles of relationship through commitment, faithfulness and permanency. Love cannot be found in the transient, the superficial and the shallow. Implicit in the human expression of vows, permanency and faithfulness was a commitment to reach the depths of another person in love which can never be achieved without continuity, reliability and predictability. What is new in our age is that the depths we are trying to reach in human relationships engage a totally new range of sexual, physical, emotional and social possibilities. *The moral crisis of our age is the need to achieve all this with one person instead of using several as stepping stones for goals which remain unfulfilled, ideological possibilities, leaving behind a trail of frustration, cynicism and corruption.* Christianity claims that the God it believes in is the full measure of love, has already realised everything and more than man can ever realise, and that human beings are travelling on a journey which is gradually unfolding in their potential of loving. But this image is shaped by God's revelation to man which insists on one to one relationships, faithfulness, permanency and commitment. Our age must be persuaded to see that, in the name of the most hallowed principles of personal freedom, it is encouraging the expediency of attempting to seek fulfilment without the necessary effort and the cross which love has always and will always continue to demand. The trivialisation of our age is not that of sex but of persons, who, in the name of rights and freedom, are sanctifying the partial, the transient, the incomplete, the shallow and who ultimately place each other constantly on the sacrificial altar of the disposable. The evil of our day is disposable relationships and our society has to retract from the abyss that it has created through its neglect of moral principles at all levels of human relationship from the pre-marital right through to repeated divorce. But the guiding principle is not to be found in sexual pleasure, either in its pursuit or denial, but in the pursuit of human integrity and wholeness in authentic intra- and inter-personal relationships.

Clearly the relative freedom from the anxieties of material sustenance which prevails in one third of the world does not exist in the other two thirds. Two thirds of the world is struggling to overcome the social and economic plight of starvation, poor nutrition and health, poverty and lack of resources and a mixture of unbalanced industrialisation in its various stages of development with the nightmares of dense population in crowded cities and towns and the neglect of the rural areas. The problem of social justice between the level of life in one third of the world compared with the other two thirds makes a lot of people focus on this social issue as *the* problem facing the world today. In doing so Christians are naturally concerned with the injustices of the prevailing standards, the use of resources and the exploitation of the under privileged. In such a discussion of social justice, love is concerned with the evils of exploitation by the powerful and the privileged and the details concern the welfare of smaller nations or of people in societies with oppressive regimes. Those who are inclined towards the left will stress the oppression and the evil of capitalism and right wing regimes. Those who are inclined towards the right will stress the oppression of communism and its attendant evils. The Roman Catholic Church has large followings in countries with both types of regime but the cry of the young has been that the Church is only too ready to attack Communism and not Capitalism because it allies itself with Conservative forces and is opposed to social justice. No one who looks carefully at the papal pronouncements of the last two Popes can really justify such a view of the Church, whatever the practical limitations in their effective implementation. The issues here are complex and not directly the concern of this book except in one respect.

This concerns the matter of population size. Many countries see as their immediate task the reduction of their population and, by such a reduction, the advance of social justice through socialist principles. Love in these countries is seen primarily in terms of social justice, which is concerned with population size, the relief of poverty, the amelioration of material standards, and the promotion of social justice, independent of race, colour or sex. Wherever these social issues predominate, sexual morality is often concerned with contraception, abortion and sterilisation. In this book the view has been advanced that the traditional objection of the Roman Catholic Church to contraception cannot be sustained although I would be in total agreement against either abortion or sterilisation as instruments of population control. Equally I recognise that contraception alone is not the answer, but simply an adjunct.

This is not to say that, in such under developed countries, the moral issues of personal relationships described as belonging particularly to the West do not exist. They do exist and will do so increasingly as the social issues come under better control. But for the time being Christianity faces different priorities in different parts of the world. The crisis of love, whether in personal relationships or in social justice, requires totally new perspectives of personal value which transcend the sexual moral principles enunciated by Augustine which have been the foundation of Christian teaching ever since. This book looks forward to a sexual morality, not influenced primarily by sexual pleasure principles but one in which person, life and relationships, both psychological and social, become the guardians of the image of God in man, by examining the ever-deepening layers of that image revealed in the spectacular changes occurring in the world today.

VIII

LOVE AND OPENNESS TO LIFE

In considering the dynamics of a new sexual ethic, Christians will want to be satisfied that traditional beliefs and convictions are recognised and integrated into the new system. Let us consider some of these deeply held convictions.

The instinctual dimension of sexuality

There is an universal belief and conviction that the root of sexuality is a blind instinctual drive which is constantly seeking physical expression and relief. This isolated biological force has always been considered as a dangerous emotional component of the post-pubertal person, particularly the man. Human beings are always capable of being overwhelmed by this daemonic quality, combining instinct, blindness, indiscriminate and repetitive expression which respects nothing else but the instinctual exigencies of the biological constitution of both sexes.

Such a view already shapes and determines the sexual expression as something intrinsically dangerous unless it is in some way redeemed and transformed. This view of human sexuality is erroneous. The relentless pursuit of sexual satisfaction would not be present if humanity did not experience a profound and penetrating joy in the realisation of physical sex.

If we analyse carefully the components of sexual arousal leading to orgasm, we can see that this contains a series of physical and psychological sequences which release an enormous amount of physical and psychological pleasure. The first phase of sexual arousal is the awareness of sexual tension, physically and emotionally, which is triggered off usually by another person, rarely by an inanimate object, sometimes by a combination of both. This arousal gives the awareness of being a sexual person and therefore confirms their sexual potential and identity. The enormous anxiety experienced at the premature loss of sexual desire and potency is indicative of the importance attached to this capacity.

The second phase is the gradual build up of physical and sexual tension involving the major physiological systems of the body. The rate of breathing, the pulse, blood pressure and other bodily systems are involved in this generalised rise of tension. The third phase leads to the ultimate release of all the accumulated tension in the orgasm. This is experienced as a sense of relief and pleasure and the consistent attempt on the part of Christianity to devalue this most basic and universal characteristic is not only doomed to failure but also betrays the authentic biblical sources which saw human sexual experience as a precious gift of God as expressed in Genesis, the Song of Songs and other references.

Thus any authentic Christian reappraisal must start with an unconditional acceptance of the goodness of the physical – psychological dimension spanning sexual arousal and sexual climax. This goodness is intimately related with life itself for human life is by definition a sexual life. The image of God is expressed fully in both male and female, the basic gender division and complementarity of humanity.

Sexual Control

The element in western society and Christianity which sees sexual activity as dangerous has one basic remedy for this. Sexual activity has to be rigidly controlled. In order to achieve this, three strategies are often employed. First, the topic is surrounded with silence, taboos, ignorance, negativity, guilt and prohibition. Secondly, the channels of expression are strictly regulated with a pronounced emphasis on the forbidden. Thirdly, in the last few centuries when Christian morality (particularly within the Roman Catholic tradition) was focused on legalistic norms, the acceptable became almost exclusively the legally permissible. This has led to a major move on the part of many people, but particularly the young, to rebel violently against the idea that what is wrong one moment can become right the next by virtue of a legal ceremony. Love does not fit into such apparently magical transformation.

Thus the interpretation of sex as an inward looking, self-centred, selfish, lustful activity has penetrated deeply into western society's consciousness and to this very day the warnings from prominent Christian men and women echo loudly and clearly that this permissive society can only find its way back to God by abandoning its evil, loose, permissive habits and returning to self-control and discipline in sexual matters.

This polemic between those who see western society abandoned to its materialistic, lascivious destruction and the stout defenders of the validity and authenticity of sexual pleasure as a justifiable end in itself, still seizes the headlines and the energy of the zealous antagonists. It is of course a futile and basically totally mistaken exchange. But, if the essential Christian truths about sex are to have a serious hearing in society, then Christianity must get its attitude not only comprehensively and fully correct but also understood as such. These truths are few but absolutely basic.

First and foremost, the Christian must be fully informed about human sexuality and educated at home and at school to be able to rejoice in it and enjoy its presence. Secondly, sexual joy and pleasure is capable of being experienced in solitary isolation but its fullness is only realisable in a relationship which is orientated towards another person. Thirdly, such relationships are overwhelmingly male-female ones. (The problems of homosexuality and other sexual variations are not being considered here.) Fourthly, the man-woman sexual relationship is primarily directed towards forming a community of life which is permanent and exclusive.

If these four basic principles are clearly recognised, then the centuries old debate about the goodness of sex will not cease but most of the heat will go out of the argument. Christians must recognise that there is a genuine but incomplete meaning in solitary and in impermanent sexual behaviour. They will have little difficulty however in convincing society that neither can become serious alternatives to the norms of permanent and exclusive relationships. Above all, a Christian community, which accepts the basic goodness of sex, its ultimate orientation towards permanent man-woman relationships, can lift the whole level of the debate from the trivialisation of sex to the trivialisation of persons and thus do justice to the roots of revelation.

Sexual control will thus become not a matter of quantitive avoidance of pleasurable sexual stimulation but of respect, in and through love, for whole persons. As a positive characteristic, it will be found in the gradual expansion of one's knowledge, understanding and acceptance of sexuality within oneself and the expression of it, in and through love of another person. The combination of the knowledge of its power and its loving potential will become the central safeguard for the avoidance of exploitation of others and of oneself. Another way of describing sexual control is the authentic integration of sexuality with life in the various phases of development of our own personality and in our relationships with others.

Openness to life

There is a passage in section 17 of Humanae Vitae which expresses the hope that responsible men and women in society will see the truth of the doctrine taught on contraception for two reasons, namely that it basically reflects the natural law of the biological procreative potential of human sexual activity, and secondly, that artificial contraception can lead to corruption of sexual standards. Unfortunately these are precisely the points which neither the world in general, nor other Christians and a substantial number of Roman Catholics can either see and understand or accept as valid. If we confine ourselves to the opposition from within Roman Catholic circles, there is of course serious objection, voiced in this book, when one part of the whole exchange is emphasised as having a supreme value, namely the biological. The encyclical acknowledges that married love has to be fully human and then proceeds to fragment the whole i.e. the physical, psychological and social by highlighting one part at the expense of the potential of the whole. Furthermore the whole basis of natural law, which is quoted as the main support of the teaching, is now under serious review by several sources.[1,2,3] Finally, the encyclical refers to the traditional dangers associated with sexual pleasure. Contraception is hinted at as a means of obtaining more sexual pleasure with less difficulty, leading therefore to less self-control. Christianity is least persuasive when it uses quantitive arguments however subtly they are disguised. The hidden warning on uncontrolled licence risks placing sexual pleasure before persons and, since both the encyclical and the whole of Christianity are concerned with persons who reflect the image of God, extreme care must be taken with the arguments used to protect this image. Christ set the standard of love in personal relationships when he placed the centre of morality in the heart and condemned the lustful look because a look is par excellence the ultimate of possible exploitation of the other who is not even *touched* but is significantly devalued because what is desired from them ignores the essentials of relationship, namely commitment and permanency.

But in another sense the insistence on openness to life is a precious insight when it is enlarged beyond the narrow confines of the biological procreative potential of every sexual act. And in what follows I want to enlarge this concept of openness to life and couple it with the experience of control and sacrifice.

Vatican II, in its section on marriage and the family has the following paragraphs: 'This love (between spouses) is uniquely expressed and perfected through the marital act. The actions within marriage by which the couple are united intimately and chastely are noble and worthy ones. Expressed in a manner which is truly human, these actions signify and promote that mutual self-giving by which spouses enrich each other with a joyful and a thankful will'.[4]

Here Vatican II, and incidentally Humanae Vitae, both confirm in unequivocal terms that sexual intercourse and all that goes with it are acts of nobility and worth, provided they are carried out in a truly human way. I want to suggest that openness to life must be seen as a much broader concept in the training and discipline of successive stages of personal growth, which will make it possible for sexual intercourse to meet the genuine human criteria set up by the Council and the encyclical.

Open-ness to life and sexual education

It has already been stated that to be a person means to be a sexual person, a man or a woman. One cannot be open to life without this fundamental orientation. Hence parents, teachers and the Church have a basic responsibility to educate the pre-pubertal child to its sexual gender and role potentiality; the neglect in the past of such education constitutes a grave defect in Christian education. This means that every home must have a plan of gradually training their children positively in the unfolding of their sexual potential, paving the way for puberty. This is an obligation which the universal Christian community has and there can be no excuse for the absence of a positive atmosphere within the home, the school and the Church towards such a sexual education and the provision of suitable material and discussion forums for the parents. Every boy and girl must reach puberty with their bodies, minds and hearts ready to be invaded by the hormonal changes which set the secondary sexual characteristics in motion.

Open-ness to life in puberty and adolescence

The above sexual education will prepare the young man or woman by inculcating positive feelings towards the changes in bodily configuration, monthly cyclical physiological changes in the woman, and above all the positive welcome and acceptance of sexual pleasure. I have already indicated that masturbation during this period is a major component of the growth of the personality. It is an openness to life which needs to negotiate two critical steps, the first is to recognise and feel that the body of the young man or woman no longer belongs to their parents but is owned by him or her and is free to be donated to and consummated with another in a relationship of love. When the Council or the encyclical refers to fully human love, a basic concept of this is the separation of the person from the parents, emotionally and physically, so as to be truly free to relate to another person. This psychological step of opening ourselves to the life of others is already grasped in Genesis 'That is why a man leaves his father and mother and joins himself to his wife and they become one body' (Gen. 2,24). Psychiatrists meet lots of men and women who cannot take this step of emotional independence and who are thus unable to commit themselves to a partner. They may remain at home, avoid company, mistakenly believe they have a vocation to the single state or pursue a life of promiscuity in which their inability to form stable relationships is a mask for their emotional dependence on parents or figures of authority. Such men and women play at being adults. They claim complete freedom for sexual experimentation and swear to their total independence which in fact they do not remotely possess.

Here real self-control and sexual discipline is to seek help to mature. It takes a lot of courage to accept that one may still be an adolescent in one's late twenties, thirties or forties, that is to say that one does not have a clear sense or possession of one's body or feelings to offer them freely to another.

The same sequence of events may result from the failure to integrate the secondary sexual characteristics and sexual pleasure with one's identity; so one's relationship with a fellow man or woman is a disjointed experience. What such a person really wants is the care and affection of mothering and fathering and has not reached their genital stage of development, so that intercourse and sexual pleasure are an irrelevance, used as little as possible, in order to get hold of a husband or wife, but, when this is achieved, what is really

79

wanted primarily is to be treated as a child, with the emphasis on nurturing not on sex, which is now rejected beyond its biological procreative necessity. In its psychological ignorance, Christianity sometimes fostered and reinforced such attitudes which are clearly anything but an opening to a life of relationship or community as one vital dimension is missing.

Once again effort and discipline are required for internal growth which recognises and allows richer sexual functioning. If this growth does not occur, the consequence is sexual withdrawal which paradoxically can take two forms. The first is promiscuity. Here the man or woman is not seeking sex but affection. However, since they are afraid that nobody is likely to give them a relationship of affection alone, they may allow sex initially and then, as quickly as possible, attempt to continue a non-sexual relationship. Since this is likely to evoke a rejection from their partner, they move on, repeating the pattern, and becoming involved in a vicious circle which they intrinsically detest. They want love and affection, but not sex, but they are forced to resort to the latter for the sake of the former. The other course is similar to the one described above. Since sex is unacceptable, they lead a single life, which may or may not be dedicated to God, but which often remains empty and arid because of their inability to form satisfactory relationships.

Summarising the problems of open-ness to life in adolescence, some moralists and liberal humanists often see the sexual activity of the young as a mere expression of pent up sexual energy and they treat it respectively by opposite principles. The first condemn the permissiveness of our age, the second rejoice in the liberal climate which allows what they interpret as the natural tendency of the young to be sexually fulfilled. Both err because they see sex as an instinctual quantitive characteristic. While pent up sexual tension certainly plays a part in such an activity, conscious and unconscious motives in various stages of pre-marital relationship are a far better guide to the ability to be genuinely open to life as a person. Life is used here as a term to indicate appropriate psychological and physical growth, acceptance of one's sexuality and identity, readiness and ability to form relationships, willingness and ability to form responsible commitment and ultimately responsible permanent commitment to another. What is needed throughout these years is not a condemnation of coitus but the encouragement, training and insight to help the young man or woman to appreciate their level of personal development, their integration of sex and personality, and their readiness for the fullest realisation of relationship.

Openness to life, to fully human life, is much more than an avoidance of fornication. Sexual intercourse can and has been avoided in the name of morality and the person can still remain appallingly immature, something which is discovered later on in marriage. So there is an essential obligation and discipline required not to use sex as a means of exploring the understanding and meaning of maturity through others. That is the way of using others as stepping-stones for one's own growth, gathering and scattering in the process the wounds of mistrust and cynicism. Does this mean that a mature person has no sexual desire and need not worry about self-control? On the contrary, the mature sexual person is open to all the joy, beauty and temptation of sexual pleasure. But their control is their maturity, a fullness of sexual being which does not need others for learning experience, but in order to share and complement. The self control lies in the fullness of sexual awareness not in its absence, for it is the latter that is the stimulus for the hunger of uncontrolled tasting.

Openness to life in the sexual life of the married

Openness to life has a strictly biological exposition in the encyclical. But we know from both the encyclical and the document of Vatican II that sexual intercourse is honourable and good. We know from the experience of married couples that successful sex is one of the most powerful means of maintaining the relationship and through the relationship, the couple sustain, heal and grow in the life they give to each other. All this indicates how vital it is to relate openness to life to the sexual exchange between the couple which makes sexual in-

81

tercourse a truly significant 'knowing' of each other as the Bible states. In order to achieve this, the whole of sexual intercourse, not a part, requires a morally mandatory care, effort and self control as it proceeds through its various stages.

Openness to life and fore-play

For sexual intercourse to be a truly human interaction, it requires that both partners are involved emotionally and physically in their preparation for sexual activity. Here countless difficulties are experienced in which, for example, wives complain that their husbands do not take enough time to prepare them for intercourse, are not sufficiently gentle, do not show affection, are ignorant of their particular erotic needs, whilst husbands may similarly complain that their wives are not interested in sex or sex play and simply want to get the act over as soon as possible, pay little attention to the preparation of sex and make infinite excuses to avoid it.

How can two people be truly open to the mutual needs of their lives if they do not know how to reach each other in this most intimate of intimate moments? The need to learn as accurately as possible the sexual requirements of one's partner and to train oneself, through discipline and effort, to provide them is an elementary requirement of love but where will the Christian spouse find this spelled out as a morally mandatory requirement?

Openness to life in sexual intercourse

The life of the partners during sexual intercourse is an expression of bodily encounter through which various characteristics of psychological affirmation are expressed. This personal affirmation does not entirely depend on the physical excellence of the act but, the more complete and mutually satisfactory coitus is, the more clearly will the couple emerge from the experience feeling that their bodies have done justice to their feelings of mutual recognition, approval and acceptance.

Successful intercourse is a most powerful life-giving experience and, of course, procreation is one of its elements of life. For reasons already extensively argued, the biological can never have the moral ascendancy or priority over the other constituents of the life-giving experience. But this does not mean that it must be rejected. Children are precious and, as the Council and the encyclical proclaim, they are the crowning expression of the community of love of the spouses. However whilst one act of intercourse is procreative in the sense of giving rise to new life *every act remains a source of continuous procreation in the sense that the life it engenders and enhances in the parents is a supportive continuation of the human life of the children.* Every sexual act is linked with new life; a very small number of these acts are linked by the principle of fertilisation and all of them by the potential quality of love generated between the couple.

Openness to life and the covenant of grace

Everything that has been written so far linking life, in the wider context, with love, self-control, discipline and effort applies to the secular reality of marriage. But as all theology of marriage[5,6] clearly indicates, marriage in the Old and New Testament, before and especially since the Council of Trent has been seen in the Judaeo–Christian tradition to reflect the covenant of grace between God and man, Christ and His Church, in fact it is a sacrament in the Roman Catholic tradition. What this means is that the secular experience of the couple is open both to express and to incorporate the life of grace, in the relationship between man and God. The case presented in this chapter for human sexuality as an essential component of life and open to the fulfilment of excellence in its various expressions is more than a compliance with a secular world that is rejoicing in the natural pleasure of sex. Long before the twentieth century, the Jewish people discovered through their prophets that marriage has the capacity, as a community of life and love, to express the relationship of life and love between God and His people. This notion was further developed by Christ and Paul in the New Testament and, with the passage of time, marriage was raised to the status of a sacrament.

What I am trying to convey here is that any sexual excellence achieved in the intimate relationship between the spouses is a fertilisation of the soil, whereby this excellence enhances the presence of God who uses these very same human characteristics to act as channels for the flow of grace. It must also be noted that the covenant of grace between God and his people nowhere relies primarily, either in the Old or the New Testament, on procreation[7] Children played a vital part in both but it is the husband-wife relationship which is used as the symbol for the covenant of grace between God and his people and between Christ and the Church. 'Give way to one another in obedience to Christ. Wives should regard their husbands as they regard the Lord, since as Christ is head of the Church and saves the whole body so is the husband head of his wife; and as the Church submits to Christ, so should wives to their husbands in everything. Husbands should love their wives just as Christ loved the Church and sacrificed himself for her to make her holy . . . In the same way husbands must love their wives as they love their own bodies; for a man to love his wife is for him to love himself. A man never hates his own body, but he feeds it and looks after it; and that is the way Christ treats the Church, because it is his body – and we are its living parts. For this reason, a man must leave his father and mother and be joined to his wife, and the two will become one body. This mystery has many implications; but I am saying it applies to Christ and the Church.' (Eph. 5,21–33)

The discoveries of our age are priceless gifts to expand the theology of marital love, as an expression of open-ness to life, life in this world caught up and divinised here and now but already reflecting the mystery of the eternal relationship of life between men, women and the Trinity.

I will conclude by specifying the role of sacrifice in this new dynamic of sexual ethics. The essence of sacrifice now is not to avoid sex out of fear and guilt but to embrace sexuality and see sacrifice as the positive effort needed at all stages of personal growth and relationship. This requires first to integrate sexuality effectively and affirmatively in one's own life and secondly to ensure by persistent effort and sacrifice that we respond accurately to the needs of those with whom we have formed a community of life. Sacrifice now shifts from being a source of repression which threatens to erupt and seize us when we least expect, leading us to the most wild and irresponsible actions but instead becomes an ever widening expansion of knowledge, understanding, acceptance of its joy and pain, fulfilment and disappointment. All the time failure needs to be seen not as an instinctual escape of control but as the need to enlarge our love of persons so that, whomsoever we let down and whatever the form of betrayal, the correction is, for the married, greater love by better sexual expression within the community of married love, and greater love for those outside it not by denying their sexuality but by acknowledging our responsibility to them that sex without commitment and permanency is unfaithfulness both to our spouse and to the third party. For the unmarried greater love means again not a denial of our own or the other's sexuality but greater responsibility by not arousing expectations without the intention of faithfulness and commitment.

The essential of the Christian message in the Old and New Testament is that human love is a reflection of divine love and its key characteristic is faithfulness to persons mediated through the permanency and commitment of relationship. The secular heresy is not a denial of love, its values or excellence, but a failure to recognise that love without faithfulness to persons idealises the transient, the incomplete, the impermanent, and ultimately the disposable. The Judaeo-Christian tradition stresses exactly the opposite. God and Christ never repudiate their love for us. That is the model of relationship revealed by God to man. That is the model of human love. In order to achieve this, ceaseless effort and sacrifice is needed.

What has been proposed in this chapter and the whole book is that a positive acceptance of human sexuality, open to life in all the stages of its development, is the appropriate Christian sexual ethic which needs as much nurturing and fostering as the ideals of the past. Now however the sacrifice and effort is directed to an enlargement of the human potential for out of this fullness not only can we love more but also our ability to empty ourselves, to make sacrifices where this is needed is much more likely to happen without the need to borrow and cheat others in and through unfaithfulness.

By shifting the theology of sex to person and love, Christian ethics thus return to the roots of revelation whereby God has revealed himself as person in relationships of love between the persons of the Trinity. Man, reflecting the image of God, fulfils this most completely when the starting point of his growth is to consider himself as a sexual person in relationships of love with other sexual persons.

NOTES

1. (For a brief comment) Soane B. 1976 *Rethinking Medical Ethics*, Clergy Review, July.
2. Haring B. 1972 *Medical Ethics*. St Paul's Publications, Slough.
3. See Chap 1 Ref 10.
4. *Vatican II Documents 1967*. The Church Today. Fostering the Nobility of Marriage and the Family. Chapman p. 253.
5. Schillebeeckx E. 1976 *Marriage*. Sheed and Ward, London.
6. Harrington W. 1963 *The Bible on Marriage*. Dominican Publications, Dublin.
7. See Ref 5 pp. 75, 86, 204.

INDEX

89

90